THAI ART AND CULTURE

The demon Punnaka with Vidhura, dated to 1813. Honolulu Academy of Art, 2961–1.

THAI
ART AND CULTURE

Historic Manuscripts
from Western Collections

Henry Ginsburg

THE BRITISH LIBRARY

First published 2000
by The British Library
96 Euston Road, London NW1 2DB

© 2000 The British Library Board

ISBN 0 7123 4620 1

Designed and typeset by James Shurmer

Printed in Singapore by Craft Print

CONTENTS

ACKNOWLEDGEMENTS

The opportunity to assemble and publish these fine Thai manuscripts and documents from western collections initially arose from an invitation to the British Library from the Office of the National Culture Commission of Thailand to produce an exhibition of original and facsimile Thai manuscripts from the Library's collection. This exhibition travelled to Bangkok in November of 1996 under the auspices of the British Council, and was exhibited for two months at the Thailand Cultural Centre. It was officially opened by Her Majesty Queen Elizabeth II during her state visit that coincided with the fiftieth anniversary of the reign of His Majesty King Bhumiphol. This volume incorporates the materials sent to Thailand on that occasion, together with other relevant examples from western collections.

Funding for the publication was provided partially by the Thai Office of the National Cultural Commission, and by two other generous grants, from the James H. W. Thompson Foundation and the Bank of Thailand.

Research for this volume was assisted by numerous colleagues, at the British Library by Anthony Farrington, Annabel Gallop, John Falconer, Dr Jill Geber, Patricia Kattenhorn, Jeremiah Losty, and Patricia Herbert, at the Bodleian Library by Doris Nicholson, at Cambridge University Library by Terry Barringer, at the Royal Asiatic Society by Dr Michael Pollock, at SOAS by Rosemary Seton, and in Thailand by Dr Kwandee Rakphong. Photography at the British Library was taken by Elizabeth Hunter.

Lastly but most importantly a debt must be acknowledged, and this work must be dedicated to, the superb artists and scribes, nearly all anonymous, who created the life-enhancing works of art shown here, happily enduring memorials to the rich cultural heritage of old Thailand.

INTRODUCTION

Traditional Thai manuscripts are fairly well represented in a few western collections, although the collections are not numerically large. Some Thai manuscripts were brought home by travellers, diplomats, scholars, and soldiers. The manuscripts in fact tended to survive better in Europe's temperate climates than in Thailand, where the combined effects of tropical heat, humidity, insects and neglect often damaged or destroyed them.

Since the earliest surviving illustrated Thai manuscripts are not older than the seventeenth century, prior developments cannot be traced. However, numerous illustrated manuscripts managed to survive from the eighteenth and nineteenth centuries. During this period such diverse sources as India, China, and Europe all left their distinctive mark on the painting of Thailand. These outside elements mixed with indigenous styles and came to form what we now regard as the 'Thai' painting style, in fact a mixture of many elements of both local and foreign origin. By the end of the nineteenth century influence from Europe had largely transformed and overwhelmed Thai painting style. And with the advent of inexpensive book printing about the same time, the Thai manuscript tradition came to a virtual end.[1]

[1] Painting in neighbouring Burma and Cambodia was also much influenced from Thailand. The forced resettlement of Thai artists in Burma after the wars of 1767, for example, radically influenced Burmese painting from this period.

1 Folding book containing Buddhist texts, mid nineteenth century. [Asian Art Museum, San Francisco]

2 Ordination ceremony for a
new monk, central Thailand.
[Photograph by the author]

Traditional Thai manuscripts are made from palm leaf or else from a sturdy hand
made paper prepared from the inner bark of the *khoi* tree (*streblus asper*). A wet pulp
of the inner bark is spread on frames to dry in in the sun in long, wide strips. The heavy
paper strips are later pasted together end to end to create a very long book which is
folded, accordion fashion into an oblong format. (fig. 1) The paper provided a good
surface for both text and illustration, and could be used in its uncoloured form, or else
blackened with soot or carbon paste. The blackened paper offers a striking background
for decorative writing and painting. (fig. 9)

The Thai palm leaf manuscript tradition is distinct from that of the folding book, and
derives from Indian palm leaf books dating from the tenth century and earlier, so the
palm leaf tradition is known to be an ancient one. It was used widely in most parts of
Southeast Asia. Due to the small dimensions of the palm leaf manuscript, it was only
really suited for painted decoration on a very small scale.

Although modern Thailand is now largely part of the global economy that reached
Asia in the 1980s, old Thailand, known to the outside world as Siam until after
the Second World War, was a land of enduring Buddhist traditions. The peoples of
Thailand include numerous ethnic and language groups, with distinct customs and
religious and artistic traditions. In addition to the ethnic Thais whose culture is
now dominant in modern Thailand, Cambodians (or Khmers), Mons, Chinese and
Indian people have all deeply influenced the culture of Thailand during the course of
its history.

The rice plains of the centre of the country and the hillier areas of the north and
south are all fertile agricultural regions, with adequate rainfall, good irrigation, and a
tropical climate. Except for the northeast, which is drier and poorer, the region was
relatively prosperous. Population was always sparse, and for centuries in the course of
warfare peoples were uprooted and moved to new places to farm the land and provide
the basis for the state's wealth.

3 Buddhist temple on the Bangpakong
River, c.1965
[Photograph by the author]

4 Large urban temple, Bangkok, c.1965
[Photograph by the author]

5 Temple mural and Buddha image,
twentieth century, at Wat Doi Suthep,
Chiangmai, north Thailand.
[Photograph by Dr. Rodney Merrill]

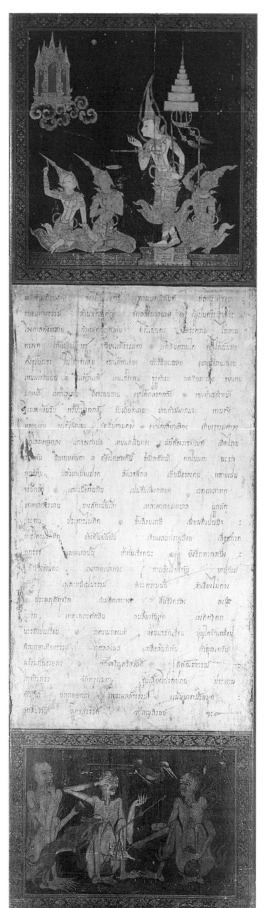

6. (*Far left*). Cloth banner painting (*phrabot*). Above, the Buddha and two disciples; Below, monks study corpses decomposing. Nineteenth century. [British Museum, Department of Oriental Antiquities, 1919.7–5.013]

7. (*Left*). Wood panel painting, showing the fate of dishonest judges, *c.* mid-nineteenth century. [Ashmolean Museum, Oxford]

Traditional social structure was largely centred on Buddhism of the Theravada school. The Buddhist temple was a mainstay of the Thai social system, with one or two large assembly halls, together with subsidiary structures such as libraries and memorial stupas, and residences for monks who were fed and supported by the local community. The support of the monks and the monastery, a cornerstone of the Buddhist faith, brings merit to the supporters. Both the rural landscape and the town views of Thailand were (and often still are) characterised by the steep roofs of the Buddhist temple. (figs 3, 4)

Sculptural images of the Buddha, often made of bronze, ranging from a few centimetres to many metres in height, are another renowned symbol of Thailand and its culture. The image serves to remind the faithful of the great life and teachings of the Buddha. He is represented mainly in the following postures referring to events in the Buddha's life: in meditation (seated with hands folded), subduing the forces of illusion which is the moment of enlightenment (seated with the right hand pointing down), teaching (standing), and in death (lying down). The images of the Buddha in bronze were modelled and cast in many styles over many centuries. The Buddha's life, and his previous lives, called jatakas, have also been widely represented in Thai painting, particularly in series of scenes on the interior walls of temples (fig. 5) in dry

8. Jujaka and his wife, from the Vessantara birth tale. Painting on wood panel, mid-nineteenth century. [Private Collection.]

9 Literary text in yellow on a black ground, late eighteenth century. [British Library, I.O. Siamese 17]

fresco technique, or on large cloth banner paintings which were made to hang in temples. Painted manuscripts illustrated these narrative scenes, and also other subjects.

Thailand was the only state in southeast Asia to escape direct control by a European power, thanks in part to effective response by the Thais, but also to fortunate political circumstances. In the crucial period of colonial development in the late nineteenth century, the French and British were preoccupied with lands to the east (Cambodia and Vietnam) and west (Burma and India), so Thailand consequently served as a useful buffer zone between their spheres of influence.

European involvement began in the sixteenth and seventeenth centuries with the growth of Asian trade on the part of Portuguese, Dutch, British, French and Danish trading ships. But trading was not easily accomplished, since the Thai king himself participated in the trade, and royal officials seriously hindered the Europeans by controlling access to the market and monopolizing the best goods. Local Thai commodities such as sapan wood, animal furs, spices, and bird nests were traded for cloth and other commodities to be sold overseas at good prices. The great city of Ayutthaya, the capital until 1767, was one of the trading centres of Asia, where the Europeans had to compete with many other traders from the Near East, India, China and Japan who all had resident communities at Ayutthaya.

In 1612 the first British East India Company ship, the Globe, arrived at 'the roade of Siam' carrying a letter from King James I for the Siamese king.[2] The account by Peter Floris, a member and investor in the expedition, of their reception and attempts to start a trading factory there is preserved in the India Office Records at the British Library in London.

Dutch traders were more persistent and generally more successful in Siam than their British and French rivals. But Phra Narai, the Thai king, welcomed Catholic Jesuit priests from France who lived and taught their religion at Ayutthaya from the 1660s onward. Thanks to Constantine Phaulkon, a Greek-born adventurer who rose in the 1680s to extremely high station under Phra Narai, the French were involved in a series of strange and dramatic events in Siam. Phaulkon plotted to bring forces from France to Siam to consolidate his own power. Louis XIV, influenced by his devout mistress Mme de Maintenon, was encouraged to believe that the Thai king could be

[2] For a comparable letter see Gallop & Arps 1991: 37.

12

readily converted to Catholicism. The French Jesuits in Ayutthaya wrote several accounts of exotic Siam that were published in France in the 1680s, read avidly by the French public, and translated into other European languages.

A number of official expeditions endured perilous sea voyages between the two lands. A Thai embassy laden with elephants and rich gifts was sent to France in 1681 and lost at sea. Two Thai envoys successfully reached France in 1684. And in June 1686 a full-scale embassy of nine Thai officials and their followers, accompanied by 300 bales of official gifts, docked at the French port of Brest. They reached Paris in August, and Versailles on 1 September where they were officially received by Louis XIV and the entire royal family. After travelling further to northern France and Flanders they returned to Brest and embarked for the return journey in March of the following year. All of fashionable France sought opportunities to meet and observe the Thai embassy. A contemporary gazette called *Mercure Galant* related their travels and activities in great detail in some 2000 pages.

The interchanges between the two distant lands were based on mutual misunderstandings, and inevitably ended in disaster. The official in charge of the royal elephants, Phetracha, seized power from the aged and ill Thai king who died in the summer of 1688. He deposed and brutally killed Constantine Phaulkon. The large French force that had reached Siam in 1687 was allowed to return to France at the end of 1688.

For the next hundred and fifty years Europe played virtually no part in Thai history. Some French Catholic priests remained in Siam, and were tolerated, and the Dutch continued their trading presence at Ayutthaya. Independent European traders, called 'country traders', continued to barter and ship goods, particularly Thai tin and lead, in exchange for cloth and firearms. (see p. 28)

The defeat and wholesale destruction of Ayutthaya by the Burmese in 1767 brought about a new Thai dynasty and new capital cities. By vigorous efforts the Thai state was revived, first at Thonburi (1767–1781) and then at Bangkok (from 1781 onward). By the 1830s the economy was flourishing and the Thais were beginning to respond seriously to the challenge of Europe, as western powers pressed more strongly for trade opportunities. Although two British diplomatic missions to Bangkok, led first by Crawfurd in 1822 and again by Burney in 1826, were fruitless, the need for accommodation with the Europeans was being recognized at the Thai court. A full treaty was finally negotiated by Britain in 1855 by John Bowring, who had made friends with King Mongkut and corresponded with him over many years. (see p. 42)

Within only a few years diplomatic and trading agreements had been negotiated with many other western nations, and a sizeable foreign community arose at Bangkok. By 1860 there were 156 European and 42 American residents in Siam, listed in the Bangkok Calendar which was published by the American missionary Dr Bradley. A number of them were described as 'in the Siamese service'. By the end of the nineteenth century the number had swelled to several hundred, with European advisors in every ministry of the moderning Thai state.

A serious crisis came in 1893 when French gunboats sailed up the Chaophraya River and threatened Bangkok, backing French demands for extensive territorial concessions. In Siam and Europe it was widely understood that the French meant to annex Siam to their existing protectorates in Cambodia and Vietnam. The British sided with the Siamese, from fear of French expansion, but offered no concrete assistance. King Chulalongkorn fell gravely ill, and the country was in a virtual state of collapse. Luckily

the king recovered, and ruled for another seventeen years. In 1897 and 1907 he sailed by royal yacht to Britain and other European countries in a semi-private capacity. In England he met eleven of his sons who were at school there, a measure of the primary role played by Britain in the modernization of Siam.

9 Typical illustrated manuscript format of the nineteenth century (above) and eighteenth century (below). [British Library, Or. 14732, and Or. 14068.]

History of Collecting

Thai manuscripts and documents first came to Europe as a result of trade contacts beginning in the early seventeenth century with the East India companies. Documents from the earliest period are rare, and include official letters and accounts by the traders themselves, and documents presented to and received from the Thais.

Some of the finest illustrated manuscripts were brought back by early travellers, traders, or soldiers. A richly illustrated manuscript showing the life of the Buddha as well as the ten birth tales, now in the Bodleian Library (36), was in fact brought to England from a temple in Srilanka in 1819. Another came to the India Office Library in

14

1824 from Burma (35), thanks to an army officer, Lt. Col. Miller Clifford serving in the Burmese wars. A Captain M'Donnell shipped a collection of Thai manuscripts and objects of many sorts in the year 1823, to Sir Stamford Raffles, by then retired and living near London, including a model of a royal barge, but only a group of musical instruments, now in the British Museum, are known to survive from this collection. The first Thai illustrated manuscript to come to the British Museum was from the hands of a sea captain at Singapore who bought it from 'a Malay or Siamese Sailor' and sent it to London via a Liverpool merchant, Mr Thomas MacGill, in the year 1844. Two early British residents of Bangkok sent back manuscripts in the 1840s. The merchant Robert Hunter owned two finely illustrated fortune-telling manuscripts that are now in the Royal Asiatic Society, London (65), and James Hayes, another merchant, acquired two important historical manuscripts, an early version of the history of the Bangkok dynasty and the history of the Mons, entitled Rachathirat, both copied by court scribes, probably at Hayes's request, from traditional Thai books, and dated 1847.

The British Museum also purchased a large album of Thai drawings at auction in 1866. The drawings in it were made to the order of Capt. James Low of the East India

7 Northern Thai mural painting, nineteenth century, Wat Buak Khrok Luang.
[Photograph by Susan Conway.]

Company, and illustrate many subjects from traditional Thai manuscript painting. Other Low items, including maps, are preserved in the Royal Asiatic Society, London.

An American envoy, W. S. Ruschenberger, was presented with a Thai fortune-telling book by the Thai prince Chaofa Noi in 1836. This manuscript is now in the John Rylands Library in Manchester (**64**).

A most important acquisition in Berlin was the superb dated Traiphum manuscript of 1776 AD which came with the scholar Adolf Bastian in the late nineteenth century.

After the Second World War a few collectors actively sought illustrated Thai manuscripts. Extensive collections were assembled by Sir Chester Beatty and by two collectors advised by the American connoisseur and silk manufacturer Jim Thompson. The first of these was Philip Hofer, a distinguished collector, curator, and bibliophile, who visited Thailand in the 1960s. His Thai collection is in the Harvard University Art Museums. A comparable collection was made by Mr. Bantli and is now in the New York Public Library. Chester Beatty employed agents to build up his extensive oriental manuscript collections, including Thai manuscripts, and they also acquired the Thai manuscripts of H. G. Quaritch Wales, the scholar of Thai history and culture. Another great collector, Henry Wellcome, the pharmaceutical manufacturer, also assembled a group of Thai manuscripts before his death in 1936, now preserved in the Wellcome Trust Library in London. It is from these collections that the documents featured in this book are mainly drawn.

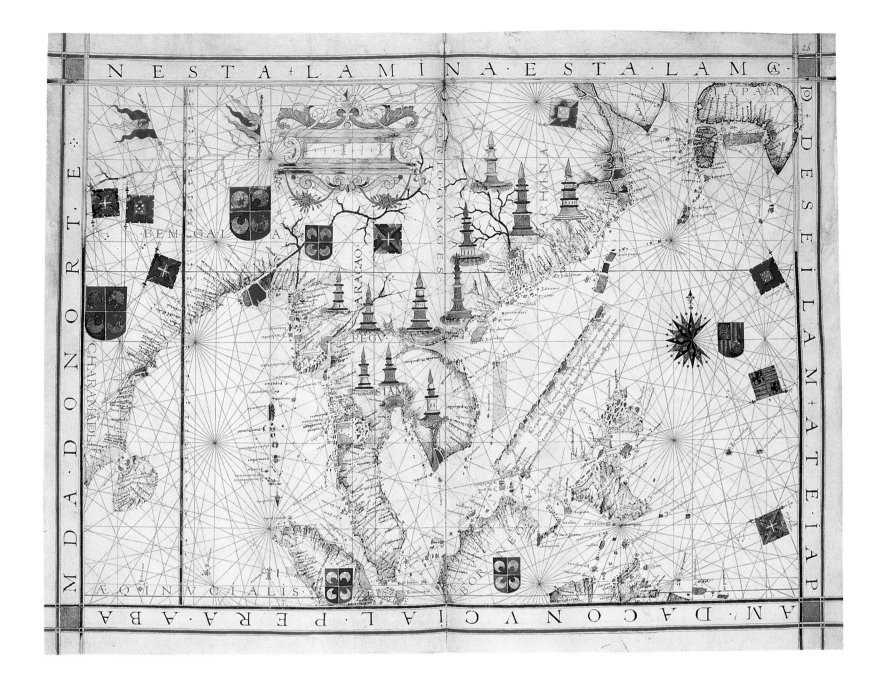

1 Map of Southeast Asia, 1575.

British Library, Department of Manuscripts, Add. MS. 31317, ff.25–26. 39 × 52 cm.

In 1575 during the troubled reign of King Thammaracha at Ayutthaya, the Portuguese map maker Vaz Dourado produced this handsome map on vellum of southeast and east Asia, one part of a complete atlas of the world occupying nearly 20 sheets. Vaz Dourado lived in India and produced a number of luxury atlases that were works of art in their own right. Rather than serving as real travel documents, they were made for rulers and merchants as artistic records of the known world.

In fact, the localised geographical knowledge in the maps was extremely limited and the map tells us almost nothing about Thailand at that time. Europeans knew little more than the coastlines of the

lands of the world they were beginning to explore, and even the coastal areas were only sketchily known. Interior regions on this map are decoratively painted, with pagodas and a few very general place names, and furnished with quite imaginary rivers, for lack of any detailed information. The text around the border indicates that the area shown covers Ceylon to Japan.

The Portuguese and Spanish were the first great European explorers and sea travellers. The Portuguese in particular settled in many Asian lands, including Siam, and remained as traders and interpreters for many succeeding generations. Portuguese was in fact the main language of communication between Europeans and Asians in Thailand until the beginning of the nineteenth century.

2 Peter Floris's Record of the Globe, 1612.

British Library, Oriental and India Office Collections. India Office Records, L/MAR/A/XIII, ff.28–29. 30 × 19 cm.

The Globe, a trading vessel of the East India Company, arrived at 'the roade of Siam' on 15 August in 1612. It was the first attempt to engage in trade with Siam. A party was sent upriver to Bangkok – six days' travel round-trip – and returned with the governor of that town who then received a letter brought from King James I to present to King Song Tham. On 17 September the Thai King gave an audience to the English party and promised them free trade and a fine 'howse of bricke.' Since damage to the ship by worms necessitated repairs, the English hired a junk for the price of 96 rupees to carry their trade goods against the monsoon flow of the river to Ayutthaya, which they finally reached only in late October.

The Dutchman Peter Floris was the writer of this account of the voyage and a capital investor in it.[1] He complains bitterly of the 'very great knaverye' of greedy Siamese officials who seized their trading goods taking out all the best merchandise for themselves. Bribes were then extracted before the remaining goods could be sold.

In fact the East India Company had little success at trading at the Thai capital and abandoned the trade post in 1623, though it was sporadically resumed later in the century. The journeys were extremely dangerous; of the Globe's crew of over 70 men, one-third died of various illnesses or drowned in storms during the voyage.

[1] Peter Floris's *Voyage to the East Indies in the Globe 1611–1615*, a contemporary translation of his Dutch journal, was edited by W. H. Moreland, London, 1934.

3 King Songtham's speech, translated into English and sent to Mr. Fursland at Batavia in Java, in 1622.

British Library, Oriental and India Office Collections. India Office Records, G/21/3A (1), ff. 130–131. 32 × 24 cm.

The Siamese king addresses his brother the 'greatt and famous King off England, my brother [sic]' via Mr Fursland, whom he takes to be 'General Commander of His Majesty's people in these parts'. He has translated the speech through his vice-king Chaophraya Phrakhlang who wrote down his words.

King Songtham writes in very friendly terms, confirming his willingness to allow the English to settle and trade in Siam, and to aid them in their enterprises. The second part of the letter tells of the disobedience of the King of Cambodia, and asks the English to refrain from trading with Cambodia until he submits to Ayutthaya. Finally, the gifts to Fursland are listed – gold cups, various boxes, a knife, a spoon, and a crown, with a record of their gold weights.

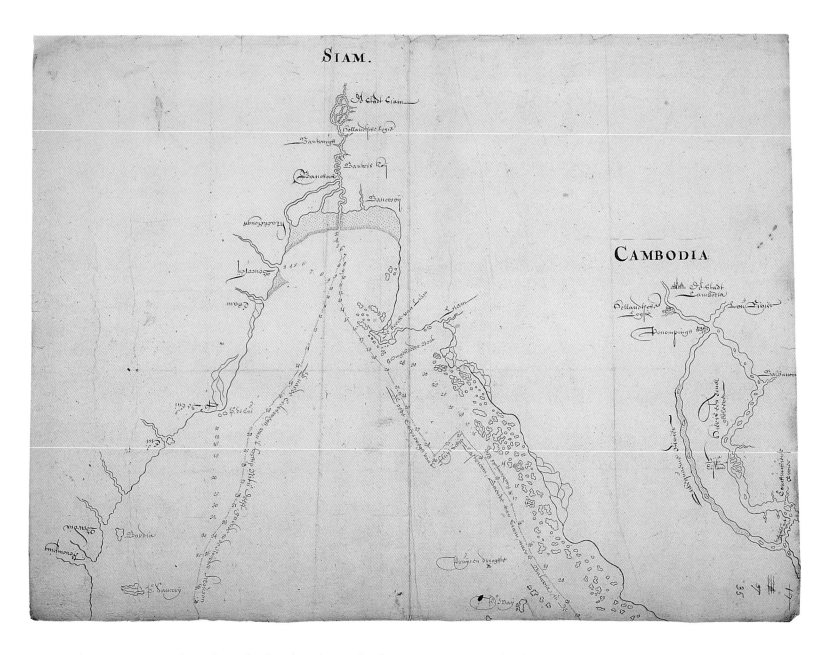

4 Dutch Navigation Chart for Thailand and Cambodia, c.1642.

British Library, Department of Manuscripts, Add. MS 5027A, f.35.
48 × 36 cm.

The Dutch, the most successful European traders in Asia in the seventeenth century, relied on navigation charts like this one for vessels travelling to both Thailand and Cambodia.

At the top of the map is the Thai capital Ayutthaya (called 'Il Stadt Siam') and below it, the Dutch settlement ('Hollandsche logie'). The location of Bangkok, then only a small town, is also marked. In Cambodia the Dutch settlement is also prominently marked, upriver from Phnom Penh ('Ponompingh'). Apart from these few features the chart indicates nothing about the geography of the region. The numerals on the chart must indicate water depths. Continuous enmity between Siam and Cambodia made it difficult for the Dutch to trade with both kingdoms.

5 King Ekathotsarot's Letter, seventeenth century.

Bodleian Library Oxford, MS. Asiatic Misc d. 3a. 64 × 26 cm.

The survival of a Thai government letter dating from the seventeenth century is very rare. Some of the text of this letter is lost due to torn parts of the paper, but enough survives for us to piece together its contents. Although the letter refers many times to the King by the name Ekathotsarot (who ruled from 1605 to 1611), the same name was also used by later kings of Ayutthaya and it is likely that this letter dates from later in the century.

It concerns foreigners in Ayutthaya, specifically the Portuguese (called in old Thai *pratukan*) and a foreign ship's captain named Kapitan 'Malaweriben'). A number of Thai officials are mentioned, Phraya Itsareha, Luang Samutsamaitri, and the 'harbour master' *cao nam cao tha*).

The letter spells out some of the terms and conditions under which the foreigners may trade and enjoy the protection of the king within a designated trading area (*khanthasima*) at Ayutthaya.

6 List of goods for King Narai, 1680.

British Library, Oriental and India Office Collections, India Office Records, G/21/7A, ff.62–63. 23 × 32 cm.

King Narai frequently ordered goods from Europe during his reign, when foreign sea trade flourished at an unprecedented level. From French records we know for instance that he ordered glass objects, 4000 mirrors, and 54 hats in a wide range of colours and shapes. Thai goods also made a great impression in Europe, as evidenced by the gifts sent with the Thai embassy to France in 1686 and the records of their reception.[1]

Cloth was a major trading 'currency' throughout Asia in official exchanges between rulers in the seventeenth century and consequently held a ceremonial as well as practical value. Six kinds of cloth, each in a variety of colours, are included in this list – Broadcloth, Velvet, Perpetuanoes, Serge, Chamlett and Bay, plus a mill to make 'tyncill' (tinsel), and a gold incense pot standing upon eagles. Since cloth terminology was quite different from today, we can not be entirely sure what all the kinds of cloth were. Cloth production depended on local raw materials and weaving methods that were specific to certain places. Most of the types requested here are probably English products. Broadcloth and Serge were English wools, as was Bay, a particular type of wool made in Colchester in Essex. Perpetuano was the name for an exceptionally durable and long-lasting wool. Chamlett (or camlet) was a fine grade of wool with special weave and colour characteristics. Velvet was sometimes made of wool and could have been English in origin, or else of silk, which was mainly manufactured in France and Italy in Europe at that time.

[1] Cruysse 1991: 392–393, 435.

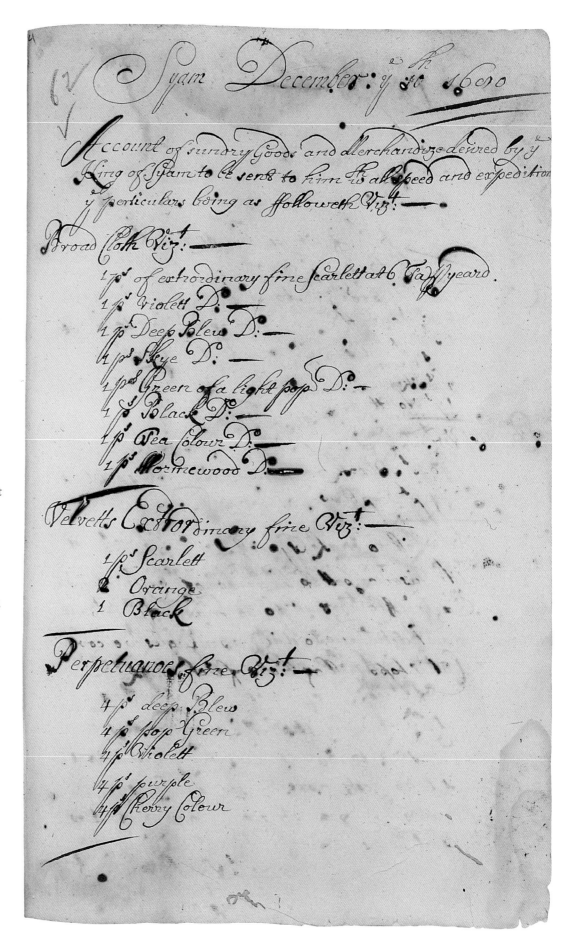

7 Letter from Constantine Phaulkon to the East India Company, December 1683.

British Library, Oriental and India Office Collections, India Office Records, E/3/43, no.5030. 32 × 21 cm.

The Greek Constantine Phaulkon first reached Siam as an employee on a ship of the British East India Company in the late 1670s. A gifted linguist, intelligent and ambitious, Phaulkon took service with the Thai king, learned the Thai language, and rapidly rose to a position of enormous power and wealth under King Narai. By 1685 he was the prime minister of Siam, in virtual control of its external trade. Residing in great luxury and pomp at two palaces, at Ayutthaya and at Lopburi, he was attended by an English secretary and a private retinue of twenty European bodyguards. (Collis 1965: 268.) In 1688 after a palace revolt Phaulkon was toppled from power, brutally tortured and killed.

In this postscript to a letter, now lost, he complains to the English Company of the behaviour of William Strangh, an East India Company agent at Ayutthaya, which was 'contrary to the stated laws of the kingdome'. Strangh was trying to make a trade agreement with the Thai court without using the offices of Phaulkon. When he failed to come to a working agreement with the British, Phaulkon turned to France, encouraging Louis XIV to hope for the conversion of the Thai king and court to Christianity.

Phaulkon's personal seal appears at the top of the page. This is the only record of his seal, which includes the small image of a falcon, a reference to his name.

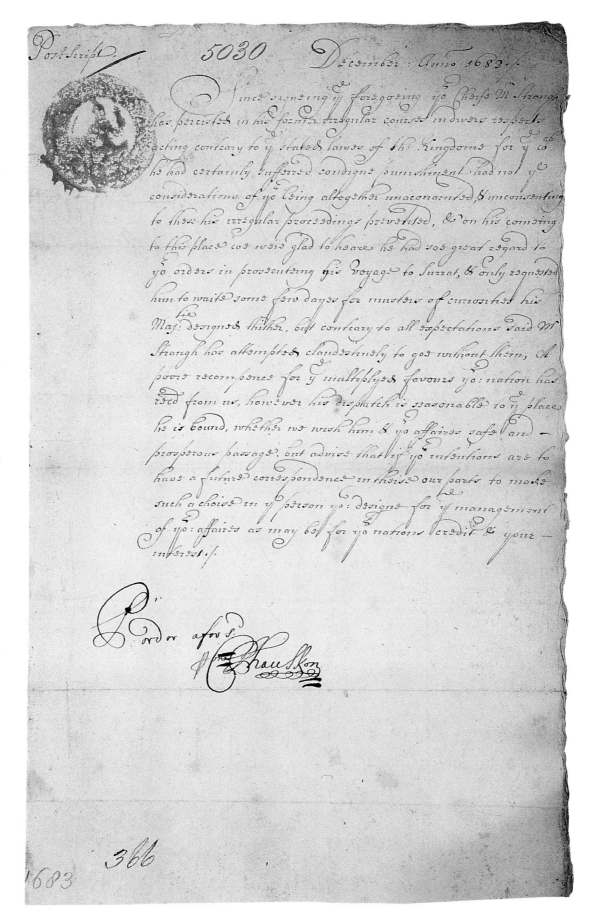

8 The Ship of Sulaiman.

Manuscript account of a Persian mission to Ayutthaya in 1685.
British Library, Oriental and India Office Collections, Or. 6942, f.1.
Written in Persian script 32 × 21 cm.

Numerous Persian traders settled at Ayutthaya in the seventeenth
century and assumed a prominent place in mercantile and political life
there. Certain families came to high political office under the Thai
kings. Indeed, the descendants of one of these Persian families, the
Bunnags, were preeminent in the Thai kingdom and its external trade
in the nineteenth century.

The Ship of Sulaiman is a unique account of an embassy sent in
1685 by the Shah of Persia to Ayutthaya at the invitation of King
Narai. It was composed by the secretary and scribe of the expedition,
Ibn Muhammad Ibrahim. The text itself is highly stylized and difficult,
thanks to the fixed conventions of theme, imagery and form current in
literary Persian of the time, but it includes many interesting details
about Thai and Persian life in Ayutthaya. It begins: 'Ship of Sulaiman,
adept at bearing travellers on the sea of true religion, over ranks of
swelling waves, through limits of confusion, till they reach the shores
of their salvation, you are the pride, the glory, the pious acknow-
ledgment of the one great King, our eternal Lord...'[1]

In 1685 Ayutthaya was a sophisticated and wealthy capital with
many foreign communities – from Japan, China, Persia, Arabia,
Macassar, Holland, England, France and others. The author praises
the Dutch for their ability as traders, and reviles Constantine
Phaulkon, the Greek adventurer who had risen to great eminence and
in the kingdom, and was in virtual control of the overseas trade.

[1] See Ibrahim 1972: 15. John O'Kane translated Ibrahim's work into English, with
extensive background notes.

9 Thai Ambassadors at Versailles, 1687.

British Library, Department of Manuscripts. Add. MS 22494, f.13. 21 × 15 cm.

A small French watercolour of Louis XIV receiving the Siamese embassy to Versailles in the year 1687 depicts three of the Thai envoys bowing before the Sun King whose throne is set above a flight of steps. According to contemporary accounts there were in fact eight steps leading up to the throne, the steps fitted with a rug or tapestry woven in a fleur de lis pattern, flanked by large silver torcheres. The ambassadors were also escorted by a dozen Swiss guards bearing the Thai sovereign's letter in a 'gilded pyramid'. Louis XIV wore a golden suit studded with large diamonds. He was surrounded by many princes and high officials, with an additional 1500 courtiers assembled in the throne hall.[1]

The small scene here is clearly very much simplified, set within an elaborate oval cartouche adorned with urns, ewers, and cornucopiae, and is only a generalized representation of the event. Eyewitness accounts report, for example, that for the most part the ambassadors remained on their knees rather than standing during the audience, and prostrated themselves repeatedly before the throne.

The embassy from Ayutthaya represented a high point of the French involvement with Thailand in the 1680s. As Constantine Phaulkon gradually rose to a position of power under King Phra Narai, he turned to the French as allies, promising them that the Thai king might be converted to Catholicism. Six French Jesuits had travelled to Ayutthaya in 1685 where they were cordially received by the king and others had been well received there since the 1660s. As a result, numerous accounts of Siam were published in France within a few years after 1685, arousing great interest in this distant and exotic land.

This was the third embassy sent by Phra Narai to the court of Louis XIV. The Thai king was anxious to pursue contacts with this great European state so far across the seas. The first embassy was lost at sea in 1681, with a large cargo of gifts including two elephants. A small mission of two Thai envoys reached France safely in 1684. And in June of 1686 the high ranking minister Kosapan reached the port of Brest with his embassy. Kosapan was a sophisticated envoy who adapted himself well to French customs, but secret negotiations were conducted behind his back by Tachard and Phaulkon who arranged to send a large French force to Thailand.

Kosapan's journey through France and the reception at Versailles were described in great detail in *Le Mercure galant*, in some 2000 pages of text during the course of their long stay in France, which were avidly read by the French public. Part of Kosapan's own account in Thai of the journey is also preserved in the French archives of the Missions Etrangères in Paris, and has been published in Thai.

[1] A more accurate representation can be seen in a contemporary engraving reproduced in Cruysse 1991: after p. 336. The procession of the 'pyramid' (in fact, an elaborate Thai throne) is also shown there.

10 A Full and True Relation of the Great and Wonderful Revolution That hapned [*sic*] lately in the Kingdom of Siam in the East Indies. London, 1690.

British Library, Oriental and India Office Collections. T 38895.
20 × 15 cm.

This account of the 1688 coup (here called a 'Revolution') in Siam was published in London in 1690. A number of French accounts of Siam had been published and translated into other European languages after 1685, and much curiosity was aroused in Europe concerning distant Siam. Consequently political events there were of great interest, especially with the involvement of the Greek adventurer Phaulkon, and the French.

As the preface to this book states, two previous accounts of Siam had appeared in London in the year 1688, one translated from the French of Chaumont and the other from De la Loubere, Louis XIV's envoy to King Narai. This account relates the overthrow of Constantine Phaulkon ('Monsieur Constant') who was imprisoned and brutally killed, and of the death of King Narai after Phetracha seized power. It is based on anonymous French letters 'never before publisht in any Language, and now Translated into English'.

Phetracha siezed the throne after a series of murders. For the fourth time in the course of the seventeenth century in Siam the succession to the throne was accompanied by violence and killings. Phetracha was an important official in charge of the royal elephants at Ayutthaya. He must be regarded as a usurper, as he had no kinship claim to the throne. Although there was resentment of the growing influence of Phaulkon and the French at the Ayutthaya court, Phetracha's motive in toppling the King, killing his two sons and Phaulkon as well, was mainly personal, a desire to seize the throne for himself.

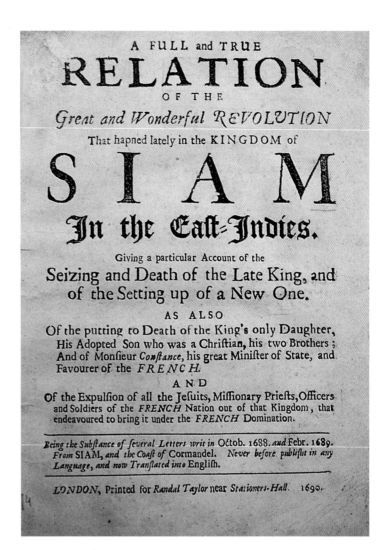

A FULL and TRUE
RELATION
OF THE
Great and Wonderful REVOLUTION
That hapned lately in the KINGDOM of
SIAM
In the East-Indies.
Giving a particular Account of the
Seizing and Death of the Late King, and
of the Setting up of a New One.
AS ALSO
Of the putting to Death of the King's only Daughter,
His Adopted Son who was a Christian, his two Brothers;
And of Monsieur *Constance*, his great Minister of State, and
Favourer of the *FRENCH.*
AND
Of the Expulsion of all the Jesuits, Missionary Priests, Officers
and Soldiers of the *FRENCH* Nation out of that Kingdom, that
endeavoured to bring it under the *FRENCH* Domination.

*Being the Substance of several Letters writ in Octob. 1688. and Febr. 1689.
From SIAM, and the Coast of Cormandel. Never before publisht in any
Language, and now Translated into English.*

LONDON, Printed for *Randal Taylor* near *Stationers-Hall.* 1690.

Fig. 7.
Ora Fluminis MEINAM.

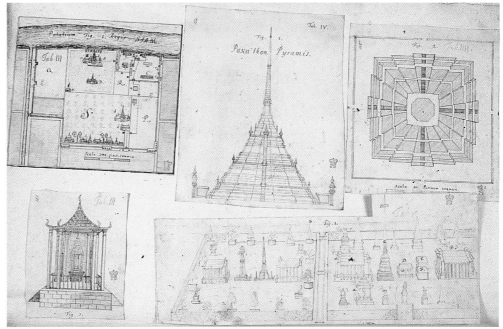

11 Engelbert Kaempfer's records of Ayutthaya. 1690.

Drawings and maps in ink and pencil on European paper.

British Library, Department of Manuscripts, Add. MS 5232.

A. River scene, no. 150 (9 × 21 cm.)

B. Kaempfer's drawing of palace at Ayutthaya no. 153 (33 × 50 cm.)

C. Kaempfer's chart of Maenam to Ayutthaya, 1690. f. 162. (31 × 18 cm)

Engelbert Kaempfer (1651–1716), a German physician and man of letters, joined a Swedish diplomatic mission to Persia in 1683 and stayed there for several years. In 1690 he continued on to Java, and thence to Siam and Japan accompanying a Dutch embassy to the emperor of Japan, reaching Ayutthaya only a year after the fall of Constantine Phaulkon and the death of King Narai.

In 1694 he returned to Europe and prepared an account of his travels in Siam and Japan, which was only published after his death. His account was translated into English, in 1727, thanks to the efforts of Sir Hans Sloane, who had acquired all of Kaempfer's papers and notes, as well as his unparalleled collection of Japanese books and paintings, which entered the British Museum with Sloane's collections in 1753, forming the basis of the original British Museum and its Library. Kaempfer's notes, sketches and maps were inevitably modified and altered in small but significant ways when they were finally published, so the original material preserved in the British Library are of great importance. [Terwiel 1989]

A. 9 × 21 cm. Kaempfer's pencil sketch of houses on the shore of the Chaophraya river is extremely natural and realistic. It was not engraved, and is the earliest landscape sketch of Thailand, dating as it does from the year 1690.

B. 33 × 50 cm. Kaempfer's original plans of the temples and palace at Ayutthaya, and drawings of temple structures, are invaluable records of the appearance of the Thai capital in the late seventeenth century.

C. 18 × 31 cm. Kaempfer's map of lower Siam from Iuthia (Ayutthaya), down to the mouth of the river. This is the original drawing, with notations in English and French. The map can be compared with engraved French versions of the same period. The engraving process inevitably involves many small changes to the original work. Inset in the upper left is Kaempfer's plan of the capital at Ayutthaya. Kaempfer has noted the site of the Mon settlement of Phrapadaeng – 'here stood formerly a city call'd Prapedain', and 'Bankok' is sited on the west bank of the river, later called Thonburi.

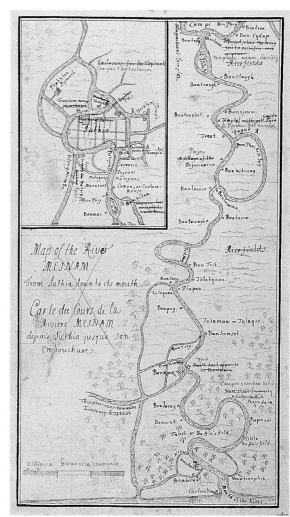

12 Thalang Letters, 1775–94.

Letter from Thao Thepkasatri to Francis Light, 1788.

School of Oriental and African Studies, London. Marsden Papers 12157A, f.33.

Mulberry paper. 38 × 40 cm.

A fine group of nearly 60 historical Thai letters is preserved at the School of Oriental and African Studies in London. It comprises correspondence in the Thai language of Captain Francis Light. Light was a 'country trader', a private merchant who lived in southern Thailand and Malaya from 1770 to 1794, mainly trading guns and silk from abroad for tin mined in southern Thailand and Malaya. Light was superintendent of the British colony of Penang after its foundation in 1786.[1]

His relationship with the local governor of the Thai island of Thalang (today known as Phuket, but then called Junkceylon, from the Malay name Ujong Salang) was a close one, and he hoped to gain control of the island for Britain. Luckily for Thailand he failed in this aim, but the Thalang rulers regarded him as a good friend, and he

helped them materially in the years of distress and famine following the Burmese invasion.

In December 1785 the Burmese attacked Siam on numerous fronts. A force attacked Thalang from Mergui, but Lady Chan, the widow of the governor of Thalang, and her sister (later honoured with the titles Thao Thepkasatri and Thao Sisunthorn) established two defensive camps, and managed to withstand the Burmese attack for a month until the invaders gave up their siege. These two ladies are honoured today as great heroines of Thai history.

The letter illustrated is from Lady Chan (Thao Thepkasatri) via a scribe, to Captain Light, early in 1788. She writes that her intended journey to the court at Bangkok had been postponed due to floods on the mainland. She says that she will make the journey soon without fail and asks Light to supply her with gifts for the King, namely guns and other small offerings. She thanks him warmly for his assistance.

[1] For a full account of the Thalang letters and their historical significance, see Simmonds 1963 and 1965, and also Kachorn 1962. A much larger group of Light's Malay letters also survives. See Gallop and Arps 1994: 131–141.

13 Finlayson's Natural History Drawings and Scenes of Bangkok.

British Library, Oriental and India Office Collections, NHD 5. WD 972/3

A. Flying Squirrel no. 762. (35.5 × 51 cm),

B. Bird Siamese fireback (bird) no. 702. (32 × 47 cm),

C. Fish nine fishes no. 736. (51 × 30.5 cm),

D. Rhizomyo siamensis (37.5 × 27 cm).

E. Gecko no. 748 (37 × 25 cm).

F. River scene WD 973. (52 × 35 cm).

G. View of Bangkok WD 972

Dr George Finlayson (1790–1823) was the surgeon and naturalist on the Crawfurd mission to Siam and Vietnam in 1821 and 1822. The mission's primary objective was to open up and promote British trade with these countries, but it did not achieve this.

Finlayson was one of the best naturalists of his day, and his studies in southern Thailand and the Malay peninsula were pioneering. He was delighted with the flora and fauna he found on this journey, collecting and sending back many specimens, now preserved in the British Museum of Natural History, as well as producing 80 natural history drawings in the India Office Collections of the British Library. A further 31 drawings illustrate landscape, people, buildings and antiquities in Thailand. Finlayson fell ill and died in 1823 on the journey home to England.

His own account of his travels, *The Mission to Siam, and Hue the Capital of Cochin China, in the Years 1821–22*, was published after his death with an introduction by Stamford Raffles (Finlayson 1826). Crawfurd's own account of the mission however was far superior to Finlayson's, published in London in 1828.

The flying squirrel was described by Finlayson in his journal as follows:

'It is altogether a handsome animal. Its flight is easy, smooth and gliding, the direction always from above downwards. Its flight in general is from the summit of lofty trees to the lower part of others, of which it soon gains the summit by successive leaps…. It is considerably larger than the domestic cat, measuring 2 feet from the nose to the insertion of the tail – or termination of the flying membrane and 20 inches from this to the extremity of the tail, making the whole length from the top of the nose to the extremity(?) of the tail 3 feet 8 inches.' [Mss Eur. D. 136 Journal, ff.7–8]

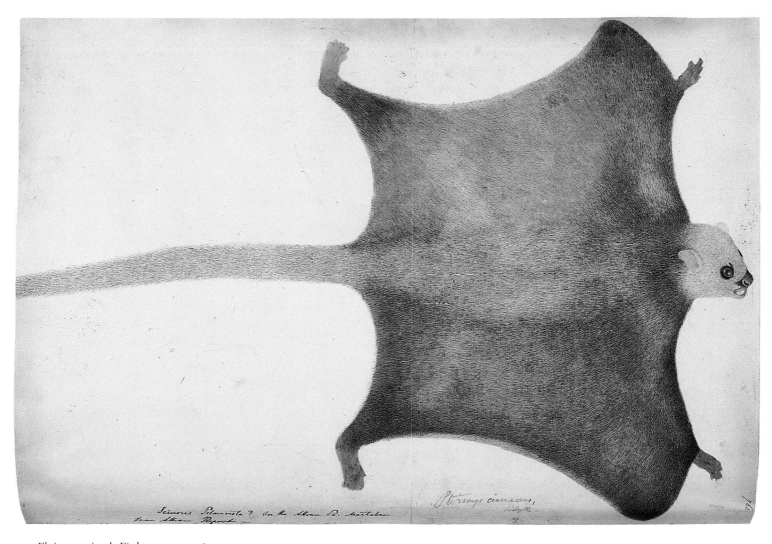

13A Flying squirrel. Finlayson no. 762.

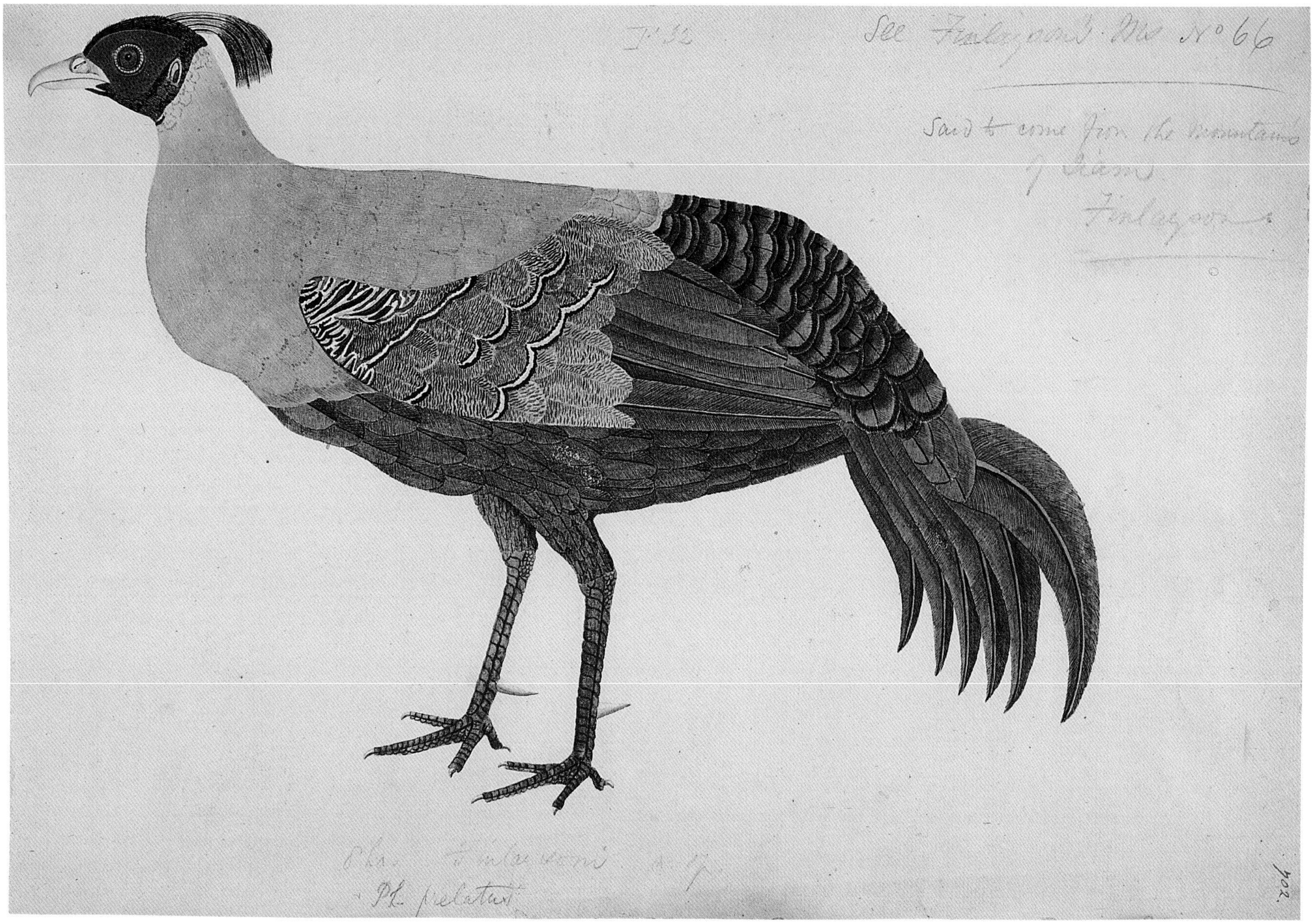

13B Siamese fireback. Finlayson no. 702.

13C Nine fishes. Finlayson no. 736.

13D Rhizomyo Siamensis.

Opposite above.
13F River scene with boats. Finlayson, WD 973.

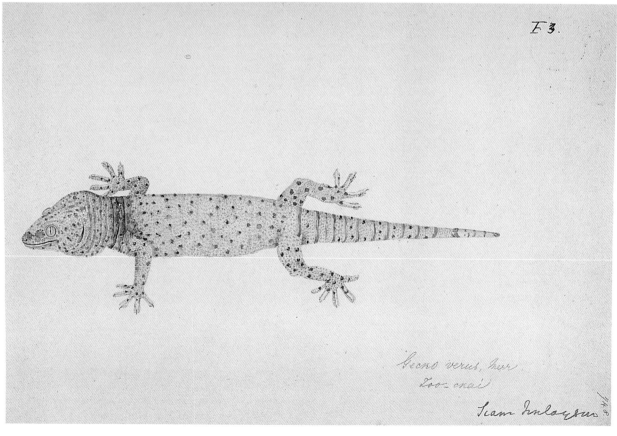

13E Gecko. Finlayson no. 748.

Opposite below.
13G Bangkok and the Chaophraya river. Finlayson, WD 973.

View of Bankok

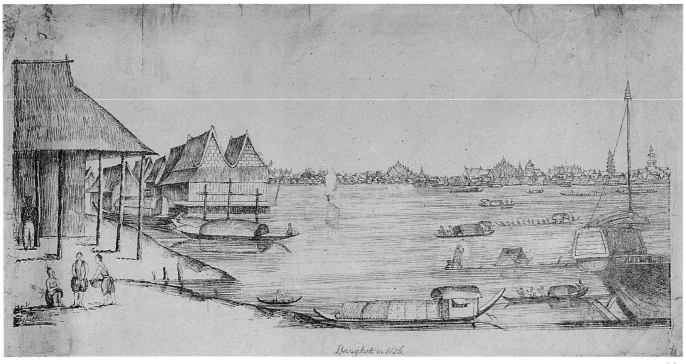

14A

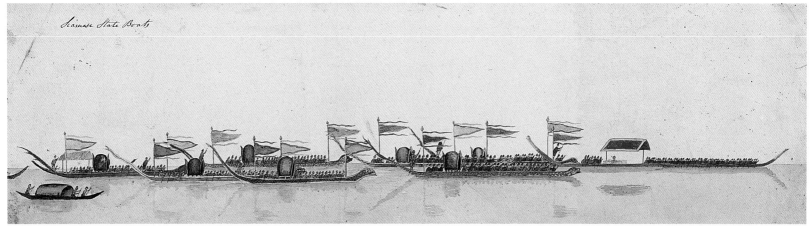

14B

14 Thai Drawings from the Wynford Album

Mixed media on European paper, various sizes.

British Library, Oriental and India Office Collections, Burmese 203.

A number of interesting drawings of Thai subjects are included in an album of fine Burmese paintings presented to the India Office in 1849 by Lord Wynford. Wynford had no known connection with Burma or the Orient, so it is not known how he came to possess this album.

A. Drawing labelled 'Bangkok in 1826' f.84. 48 × 24 cm.
Another drawing like this one in the Wynford album is labelled 'lithographed at Ava by JB', so this one was probably also made there by the same hand. It is a somewhat generalized view of Bangkok from the west side of the Chaophraya river, showing the royal temples.

B. Siamese State Boats f.29. 57 × 15 cm.
The elaborate royal barges of old Thailand were impressive in size and with elaborate decoration. Special music accompanied the rowing of

the great boats. It is known that a 15-metre model of such a barge was sent to Sir Stamford Raffles in England in the year 1823, but its whereabouts today is unknown. On major state occasions the royal barges are still used on the Chaophraya River in Bangkok.

C. White Elephant of Siam f.30. 33 × 21 cm.
The white elephant was a symbol of the prosperity of the Thai kingdom, and captured specimens were kept in splendour at the court.

D. Wat Pho and steamboat, seen from the west side of the Chaophraya River. Photograph. Late 1860s. (Private Collection, London.)

This rare photograph dates from the very beginning of King Chulalongkorn's reign and depicts the royal temple called Wat Pho. James Thompson made a photograph of the same subject from a similar high vantage point above the river. This small photograph is probably not the work of Thompson. There were numerous photographers working in Bangkok in the 1860s.

White Elephant of
Siam (*top*).
Wynford album,
I.O. Burmese 203.
British Library,
Early photograph
of the Chaophraya
river (*right*).
Late 1860s.
(Private collection.)

14D

15 James Low's Maps of Siam.[1]

Map of Siam Camboja and Laos, 1824 [Compiled by Capt. James Low, copied by A. J. Fransiz.]

Hand drawn map on European paper, 71 × 92 cm.

British Library, Oriental and India Office Collections, X/3327.

While serving in the East India Company in northern Malaya and Penang, Captain James Low compiled a map of Thailand, Cambodia and Laos in the year 1822, basing the outline on D'Anville's Atlas (published in 1780 and previously) and adding information from other sources including local Thai maps. Low submitted his map to the East India Company at Penang in April 1824 and was awarded the considerable sum of $2000 (in Spanish dollars) for his efforts. A revised map of the same area was made by Low in 1830.[1]

In the early nineteenth century most of Thailand was still quite unexplored. Even the coasts, the areas most frequented by foreign travellers, were ill-defined. Low's map was based on second-hand information that he gathered from various sources, and inevitably much of it was highly inaccurate. Nevertheless it is a valuable summary of the limited knowledge of the area at that time.

One of the more serious errors in his map represents the Songkhla lake (in Thai, Thale Songkhla or Thale Luang) as a large bay running inland from the sea at Songkhla. In fact the 'lake' is a lagoon that runs first inland and then to the north, leaving a narrow peninsula comprising the east coast. It is likely that he based this version of the Songkhla lake on a contemporary Thai map. A surviving Thai map of the peninsula dating from this period depicts the Songkhla lake quite as Low does on his map, omitting its northern extension. Similarly Low's depiction of the upper course of the Mekong and of the headwaters of the Chaophraya River is also wholly inaccurate, and may be based on schematic representations also shown on contemporary Thai maps.

Low added the following information: 'This map was compiled in the year 1822 and has since been enlarged. The Outline of this Map has chiefly been taken from D'Anvilles Atlas. The latitudes and longitudes of the principal places upon which the construction of the Map depends have been mostly laid down according to more recent Geographers. In several Charts which were not then compared with this one by the Compiler, the positions of the following places are thus assigned.... But the coasts of the gulf of Siam have never been accurately surveyed and a general Sketch only is here attempted.'

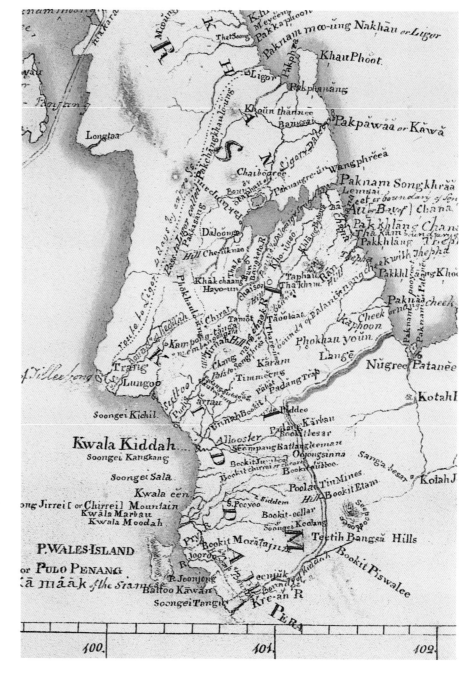

[1] For a complete study of Low's Thai maps, see Sternstein 1985 and 1990.

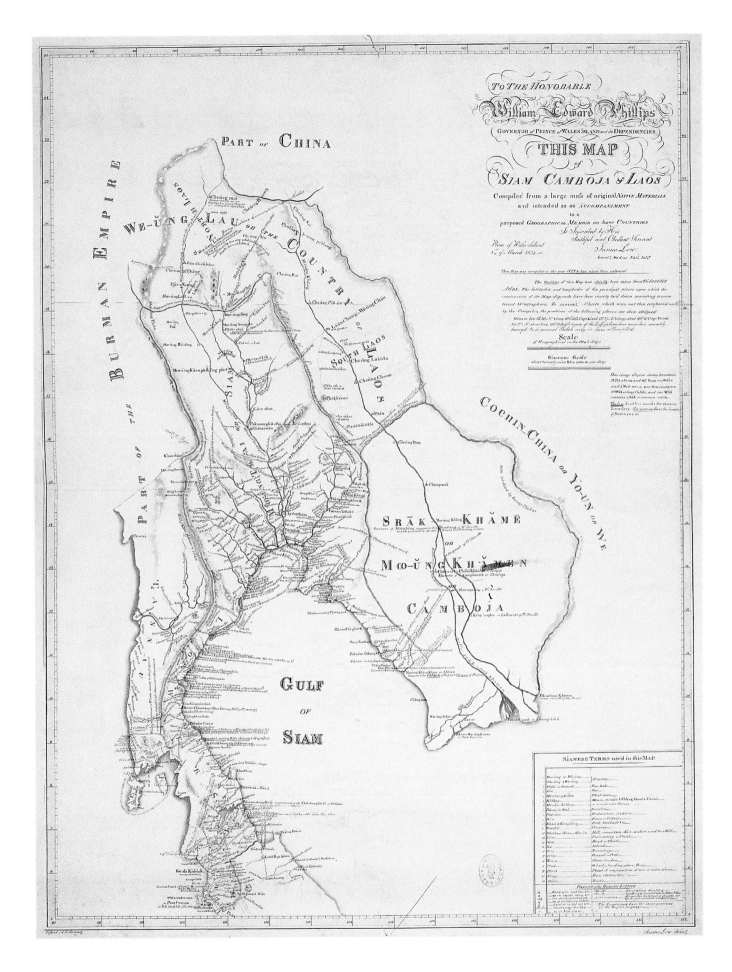

16 Henry Burney's Map of southern Thailand, 1820s.

Royal Commonwealth Society Collection, Cambridge University Library.

Hand drawn map on European paper.

Henry Burney was born in Calcutta in 1792, a grandson of the renowned English music scholar Charles Burney. By 1818 he had joined the East India Company and was serving in Penang. He spent the next decades actively involved in Malay, Thai and Burmese affairs.

Burney learned the Thai language, and negotiated with Thai officials on a number of delicate issues. In 1825 he was appointed Political Agent to the Siamese States, and went to Bangkok to improve relations with Siam, to open better trade terms for the British, reassure the Thais regarding British activity in Burma, and to negotiate the return to Burma of Burmese civilians from Tavoy and Mergui who had been forcibly moved to Thailand by marauding Thai soldiers. Forced migration was a standard feature of warfare in Southeast Asia from time immemorial, so the Thai would have had little inherent sympathy for Burney's objections to the treatment of the Burmese, especially as the Burmese were hated after many centuries of invasion of Thai territory. Nevertheless Burney succeeded in returning many hundreds of the Burmese to their homes, an early instance of humanitarian intervention in modern history.

Burney was granted an audience by the new King, Rama III, who invited Burney's six year-old son as well. Robert Hunter, the English merchant resident in Bangkok at that time, was also present and several interpreters completed the British party.[1] Questions and answers were relayed through a succession of court officials, one of whom was the official interpreter. The British were regarded by the Thai with greater suspicion than at any other time in their mutual history, for the subjugation of Burma, bitter enemies to the Thai, led the Thai to fear that the British would try to extend their domination to Thailand as well.

Burney's hand-drawn map, like Low's, is a summary of the limited state of knowledge of Thai geography in his day rather than a complete map. He has added notes on the various states of southern Thailand, identifying the Thai rank of the local ruler of each state.[2]

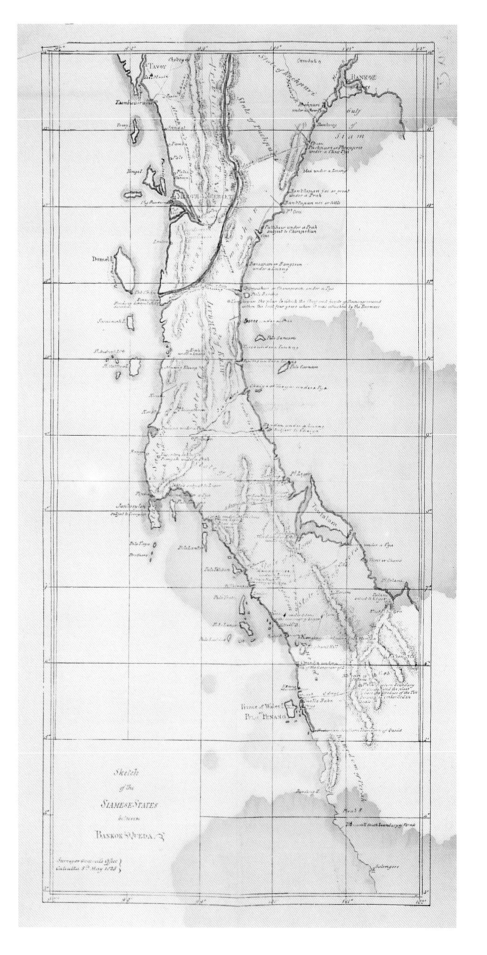

[1] Burney's Papers are held at Cambridge University Library in the Royal Commonwealth Society Collection. For a description of them by David Wyatt see Blackmore 1985.

[2] Hall 1974: 99–123.

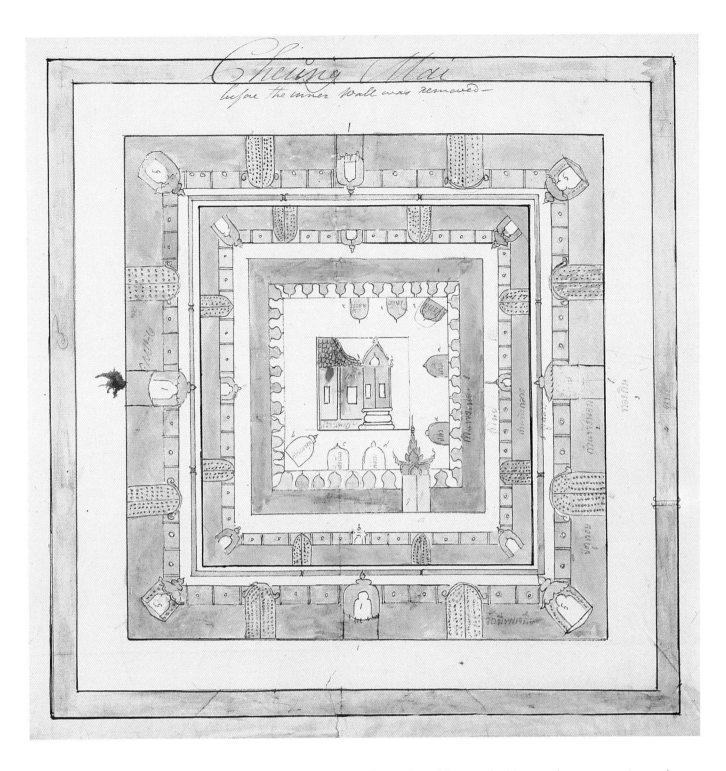

17 Map of Chiangmai, *c.*1820.

British Library, Oriental and India Office Collections, India Office Prints and Drawings, WD 1750. 48 × 37 cm.

This rare map of the old walled city of Chiangmai came to the India Office with the Finlayson collection and can be dated to *c.*1815–20 from its watermark. The original city was square with an enclosing wall and moat. Each house in the old city was set in a spacious garden with fruit and palm trees.

Chiangmai was the centre of the northern Thai kingdom of Lanna until it became part of the Bangkok kingdom in the late nineteenth century. The northern kingdom had its own language, script, and religious traditions, which were all distinct from those of the centre.

Ralph Fitch, an English merchant, visited Chiangmai in 1587 and wrote of its prosperous markets. But its isolated location, six to eight weeks' journey by river from Bangkok (and three weeks downriver going back), meant that Chiangmai would never engage in extensive international trade.

Many wars with Burma in previous centuries resulted in a common defensive policy that eventually united the north and south of Thailand.

18 The First Book Printed in Thai in Thailand, 1837.

Christian Tract (ruang phrasasana) and History of America.

British Library, ORB 30/ 894, and Siam 41. 13 × 20.5 cm.

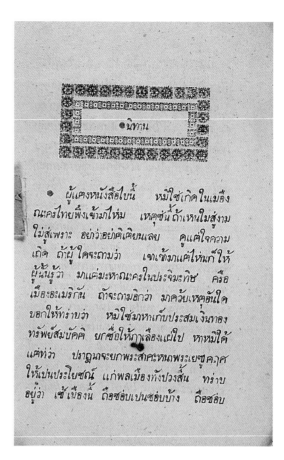

The earliest known printing in the Thai language was made by French catholic priests in 1796, but the script was romanised rather than in Thai letters. (Duverdier 1980: 209). In the early nineteenth century American and British missionaries became active in Thailand. In 1819 Thai script was printed at Serampore near Calcutta. American and British protestants had begun printing there in numerous Asian scripts in order to teach their faith more widely.

The Thai type fonts made near Calcutta were used in Captain James Low's *Grammar of the T'hai or Siamese Language*, published at the Baptist Mission Press in Calcutta in 1828. The Thai script in this first grammar of the Thai language is hard to read, and full of errors compared to modern spelling (though Thai spelling was in fact haphazard until it was reformed and standardized in the late 19th century). From 1823 the missionaries were printing in Thai script at Singapore, and when in 1836 the American Dr Dan Beach Bradley settled in Bangkok he brought with him Thai print font. Dr Bradley made a great impact in Bangkok, introducing vaccination against smallpox, as well as printing the first books in Thai. He was a respected friend of King Mongkut during the 1850s and 60s. The British Library is fortunate to possess a copy of an 1837 Thai printing from the Mission Press in Bangkok, probably the work of Charles Robinson of the American Board of Commissioners for Foreign Missions. A handwritten inscription on it reads 'Mission Press, Bangkok 1837'. The preface explains in far from perfect Thai that the foreign church men had come to Thailand not to find gold and riches but to teach the good word of Christianity.

Another charming book apparently from the same press is a history of the United States composed by one of the American missionaries and entitled *Ru'ang rao phongsawadan Amerikan*. Shortly after 1845 J. H. Chandler, an American missionary colleague of Dr Bradley who was expert at all forms of mechanics and construction, fashioned new and improved type for printing Thai. At the same period Prince Mongkut was also creating a Thai printing font.

Dr Bradley's press was destroyed by fire in 1851, but in the following year with the support of King Mongkut, Bradley established his new printing press at the mouth of Bang Luang Canal, and there he printed a number of Thai historical, legal and literary texts.

19 The 'British Museum' Chronicle, 1807 and 1847.

British Library, Oriental and India Office Collections, Or. 11827. 13 × 21 cm.

A major text of Thai history was discovered in the British Museum Library in 1958 by the Thai historian Khachon Sukhaphanit. It is dated to 1807, in the reign of King Rama I who tried to preserve the contents of the literary, religious, legal and historical documents of Siam lost in the destruction of Ayutthaya in 1767.

This copy of the historical text, in black ink on blue European paper, was made from a set of 30 Thai folding books which were subsequently lost. It preserves one of the oldest surviving versions of Thai history, which is more complete than any of the versions produced in the reign of King Rama I. The copy was apparently made for the Englishman James Hayes of the English Factory at Bangkok in 1847, as indicated in a companion volume [Or. 11828] copied by the same scribe or scribes, containing the Rachathirat, history of the Mon peoples. This companion volume contains James Hayes's name and seal, and the date 1847. A third matching volume contains a manuscript dictionary of the Thai and English languages. The manuscript of the 'British Museum chronicle' was given to the British Museum in 1948 by Hayes's descendants.[1]

[1] Prachum phongsawadan phak 82, Phraratchaphongsawadan krung Sayam chak ton chabap khong British Museum krung London. A printed version of this text appeared in 1964 and 1994, published by the Kaona Press and again by the Thai Fine Arts Department. A facsimile of the text was published by Toyo Bunko in Tokyo, edited by David Wyatt, as *Chronicle of the Kingdom of Ayutthaya, the British Museum version* (Tokyo, 1999).

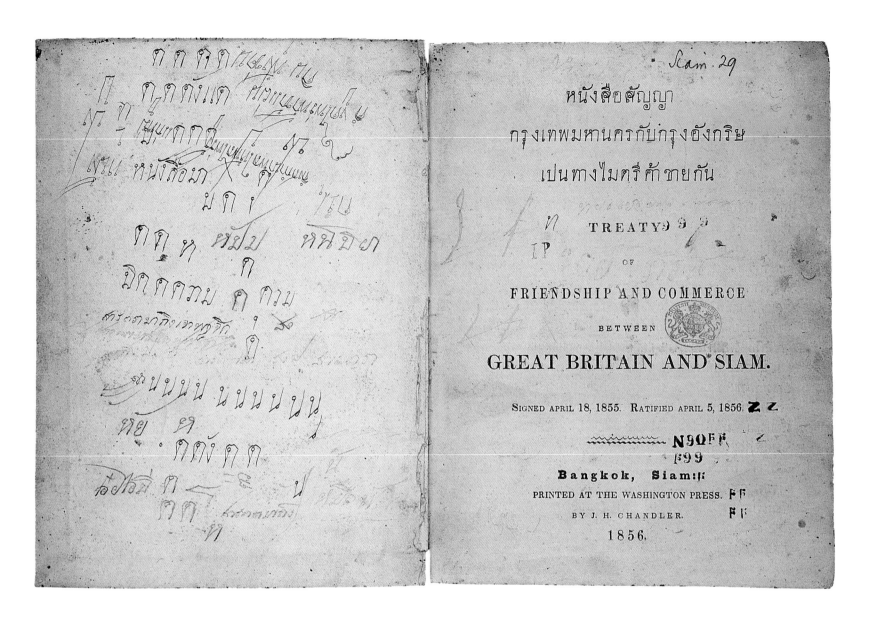

20 The Bowring Treaty, 1855–6.

Text of the Treaty, in Thai and English, printed in 1856 by the
Washington Press, Bangkok, by the American missionary J. H. Chandler.

British Library, Oriental and India Office Collections, Siam 29.
23 × 17 cm.

An agreement for trade between Great Britain and Siam providing
favourable rates of duty for British merchants was only concluded in
1855, despite the previous attempts of Crawfurd in 1821, Burney in
1825, and Brooke in 1850. The Bowring treaty of 1855 spelled out
export duty on 64 commodities, including ivory, rhinoceros horn, an
array of animal bones and hides, ray skins, hemp, dried fish, sapan
wood, rosewood, ebony, and rice. The treaty gave the British rights of
residence and an extra-territorial legal system administered by a
British consul in Bangkok.

This is a rare surviving copy of the treaty text, in Thai and English,
printed by the American missionary J. H. Chandler. It belonged to
Bowring himself, and came to the British Museum after his death in
1872. Sir John Bowring (1792–1872) was serving as governor of Hong
Kong when he was comissioned to negotiate with King Mongkut and

his government. Bowring was a brilliant man of letters of his day who
wrote and translated widely on many literary topics, and knew fifteen
European languages. In Hong Kong in 1857 he was poisoned, along
with many other British residents, when arsenic was put in the bread.
His wife did not recover from the attack and died in 1858.

Bowring formed a personal friendship with King Mongkut, and
corresponded with him until the king's death in 1868. The friendship
was no doubt a factor in the forging of the treaty, but court factions
had great influence, probably greater than the King's own. On the
British side the negotiations were carried on by Bowring accompanied
by his son John, and Harry S. Parkes, British consul to Amoy, and on
the Thai side by the powerful Bunnag family. [Terwiel 1983: 175].

To lessen the danger of offering trade privileges to a single
European power the Thais soon concluded treaties with other
European states. But the British were the primary traders in Siam for
the duration of the nineteenth century. An English tutor, Mrs Anna
Leonowens, was engaged to teach the young heir apparent who
became King Chulalongkorn in 1868, together with other royal
children, so that British education became a standard for the Thai
elite.

21 Bishop Pallegoix's Map of Thailand, published in 1854.

British Library, Oriental and India Office Collections, India Office Map Collection, x/3329. 41 × 56 cm.

By the year 1854 considerable progress had been made in the mapping of Southeast Asia, compared to the pioneering works produced by Crawfurd, Burney and Low in the 1820s (**15**, **16**). This 1854 map was published by Monseigneur Pallegoix, the learned French Bishop of Mallos who was the head of the Roman Catholic church in Siam, and a distinguished scholar of the Thai language and culture. His Thai grammar (1850) and dictionary (1854) are among the best works of their kind from any period. He also published a general account of Siam in which these maps appeared. Pallegoix's map incorporates inset maps of the city of Bangkok.

By the middle of the nineteenth century trained surveyors, working for both Europeans and the Thais, were beginning to map the mainland of Southeast Asia systematically. The Thai chronicle of the Fourth Reign for example records that a British surveyor named 'Doichok' was working for the crown in the 1860s (Flood 1965: 368) By the end of the century however there was still a great deal left to do, and James McCarthy spent twelve years producing his records of the interior areas (**32**).

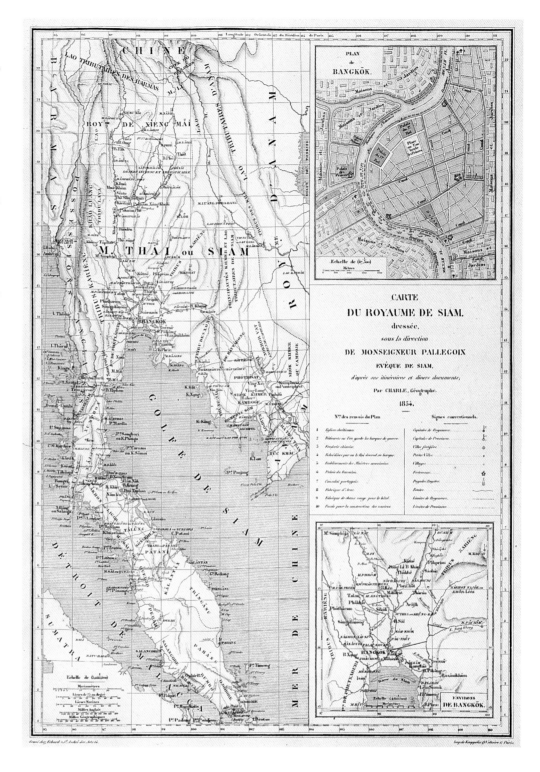

22 Henri Mouhot's papers, 1858–61.

British Library, Oriental and India Office Collections, Or. 4736.

Henri Mouhot, an intrepid French scholar and naturalist, was considered the 'discoverer' of Angkor Wat, the great twelfth-century Cambodian temple. In truth, Angkor had been visited continually over the centuries from the decline of the Cambodian empire in the fourteenth century, and Mouhot never made any claim to have 'found' it. But his description of Angkor after his visit there in 1859, published in England and France in the 1860s, first awakened Europeans to its greatness as one of the wonders of the world. Very soon after, the British photographer John Thomson made pioneering photographs at Angkor and published them in his *Antiquities of Cambodia* in Edinburgh in 1867. The Angkor region actually lay within Siamese territory from the end of the eighteenth century until 1907 when it was ceded to France.

Born in France in 1826, Mouhot worked for ten years in Russia as a tutor, and came to England in 1856 with his brother Charles and their wives, both nieces of the distinguished British explorer of Africa in the late eighteenth century, Mungo Park. The two couples settled in Jersey. Upon reading a book on Siam, doubtless Bowring's *Kingdom and People of Siam* of 1857, Henri Mouhot determined to travel there to study natural history. He convinced the Royal Geographical Society in London to sponsor his expedition although he had to pay for it with his own funds. For the next four years Mouhot made four extremely arduous journeys from Bangkok, to the southeast and northeast of Thailand, to Cambodia, and Laos, studying insects and animals, ethnology and archaeological remains. His health was good over the period of his travels through dangerous areas, but in Laos Mouhot fell seriously ill and died in November 1861. His diaries were returned to his brother in England, where they were selectively edited and published with Mouhot's own illustrations, first in the French magazine *Tour du Monde* in 1863, and in English translation in 1864. A French edition, with a number of differences, appeared in 1868.[1]

Some of Mouhot's papers were donated to the British Museum late in the nineteenth century, including three handwritten passports issued in Bangkok in Thai and Cambodian authorizing his travels. In a letter to his brother of October 1860 Mouhot described how difficult it had proved to obtain travel documents for the journey to Laos.

The passports that were preserved, issued the same year, instruct local headmen to assist Mouhot and his party, supplying them with provisions and carts for travel. Mouhot explains in his diary how the instructions were often of no use when no one could be found to read the instructions, or when no carts or oxen were available.

Mouhot meticulously copied out the first five lines of the ancient Thai stone inscription of King Ramkhamhaeng which had only been discovered a few years previously at the ancient Thai capital of Sukhothai. Mouhot dates it in his note to 1193 AD, but 1193 is in fact a date appearing in the inscription from a Thai era system, and not in the Christian era. Below the lines from the inscription Mouhot illustrates numerals found in the Sukhothai inscription, and another inscription from Kamphaengphet. Mouhot's inquiring mind led him far into the languages and culture of Siam, Cambodia and Laos.

23 John Thomson, F.R.G.S. The Antiquities of Cambodia, Edinburgh, 1867.

The First Photographs made at Angkor Wat – albumen prints from glass negatives.

British Library, Oriental and India Office Collections, X. 415.

Only a few years after Henri Mouhot's journey, another intrepid traveller visited Angkor Wat, this time with an intention of making photographs of it. The art of photography was only 30 years old in the 1860s and the necessary equipment was still extremely cumbersome. The Scot John Thomson (1837–1921) was a pioneer in recording the peoples, monuments and landscapes of the orient, and he spent several years in China and Southeast Asia. After several years photographing in China, Thomson passed six months in Thailand before setting off in January 1866 on the arduous journey by river and overland to Angkor with his photographic equipment in 'two wretched buffalo carts and a pair of ponies', accompanied by Mr Kennedy of the British consulate. He had to ignore grave warnings of the dangers of sickness and wild animals *en route*.

To produce the wet-plate collodion photographs, ten porters were required just to carry the necessary equipment. Glass negatives in two sizes were produced from this process in a portable darkroom. In one continuous process the glass plate was coated with the collodion to which the light-sensitive silver nitrate was added, the plate was exposed for a minimum of five seconds, and then fixed. The chemicals had to remain moist during the entire process, so interruptions could spoil the result. The arduous process was much faster in exposure time than the previous calotype technique, and when well controlled the photographs were fine in detail and tonal range. Albumen prints on paper could be produced later in a proper darkroom.

Photographing over several days at Angkor, Thomson was at times plagued by 'a tribe of black apes, wearing white beards' whose antics on the overhanging trees spoiled some of the photographs.[1] The India Office Library copy of Thomson's book published in Edinburgh in 1867 contains 24 extra photographs to the sixteen printed for the regular edition, and some of the smaller size albumen contact prints are reproduced opposite.

A. f. 30. Part of the central tower, 8 × 9 cm.
B. f. 32. The seven headed Snake, 8 × 10 cm.
C.f. 39. Huts at Nakhorn Wat, 8.2 × 9.3 cm.

[1] See Mouhot 1966 and 1992.

[1] Thomson 1875: 151–2. Ovenden 1997.

Henri Mouhot's passport (*top left*). British Library, OR. 4736.
Mouhot's copy of a stone inscription (*below left*). British Library, OR. 4736.
Central tower of Angkor Wat in 1857 (*top right*).
Seven headed serpent at Angkor (*middle right*).
Huts at Angkor, 1857 (*below right*). British Library, X.415.

24 King Mongkut.

Carte de visite photograph, 1868 and Royal letter, 1869.

British Library, Oriental and India Office Collections, Mss. Eur. G/38/11, f.17d.

6.5 × 10.5 cm.

King Mongkut presented this photograph in the last year of his life to Sir John Bowring and inscribed it on the back:

'S. P. P. M. Monkut was born on 18th October 1804, crowned in 15th May 1851 and reigning on the year 1868 being 18th year of his reign & 64th year of his age when this photographic view was taken.'

The initials SPPM stand for the the Thai royal title 'Somdet Phra Boromma Maha'

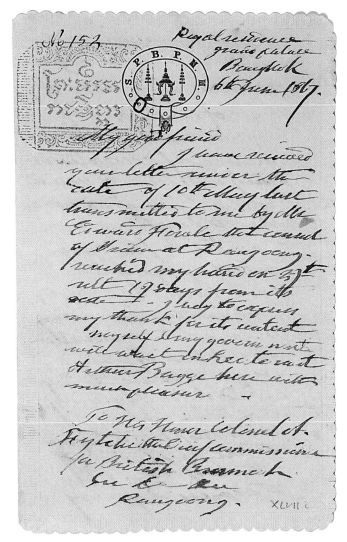

25 Letter from King Mongkut to Colonel Fytche in Rangoon, 1867, with yellow silk envelope.

British Library, Oriental and India Office Collections, Mss. Eur. G/38/11, f.17k.

8.8 × 13.6 cm.

The King thanks Col. Fytche, the chief Commissioner for British Burmah … Rangoon, for a book on decorations and insignia, and complains of a painful cancer in his right leg. The letter is dated 6 June 1867 at the Royal residence, Grand Palace Bangkok. It survives with its original yellow silk envelope.

The text begins: 'My good friend, I have received your letter since the date of 10th May last transmitted to me by Mr Edward Florale the consul of Siam at Rangoon. Reached my hand on 27th ult.… I beg to express my thanks for its content. Myself and my government will wait in [hec?] to meet Arthur Bagge here with much pleasure

I have had received long while ago the large book concerning code of honor of every one of Eupean [i.e. European] nation & various manner of decorations being insignia of various classes. And also your arm(s) to be attachd or cemented in first page or title page of the said book on which I have some according to your late instruction for a token of your remembrance in my hand and for showing the honor of being on friendship with you to all spectators of that book. I beg to express my very sincere thanks to you for the same.

Now I am sick of painful cancer in my right leg can not stand up can not walk to anywhere but I hope I will be well in health on next month. You can learn fully about my sickness from my consul Mr Edward Florale who is now under your protection.

I beg to remain your faithful good friend S. P. P. Mongkut'

The monogram in roman letters on the paper reads S P B M M, standing for the royal title 'Somdet Phra Boromma Maha Mongkut'. The seal next to it in Cambodian letters reads 'phraborommaratcha-ongkan', meaning 'royal statement'.

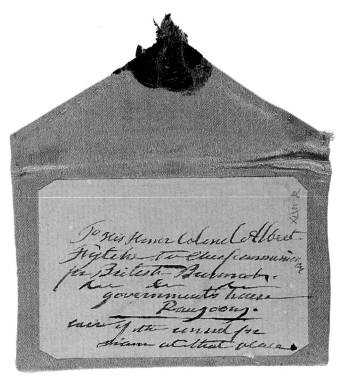

The blessing curious she Elephant, of which the representation of likeness annexed herewith, was apprehended at the jungle of Radee in Eastern province of the Laos city named Yasodhon, which is dependant & tributary to Siamese authority. The apprehension of the animal took place on Monday 1st May 1854, which is the ending part of the third year of the reign of His present Majesty Phra: Bard Somdetch Phra: Paramendr Maha Mongkut, the king of Siam and Sovereign of Laos &c; and has been remained at "Yasodhon" 9 months during rainy season, and was conveyed from thence on February 1855, and safely arrived at Bangkok on 8th March 1855, which is yet the 4th of the present reign. The Elephant is 6 feet and 4 inches in her height.

26 King Mongkut's Elephant.

Coloured drawing on European paper, 1855.

British Library, Oriental and India Office Collections, India Office Mss. Eur G/38/11, xlv. 32 × 34 cm.

King Mongkut presented this picture to Sir John Bowring. It is a coloured drawing, and an account of his royal elephant. Below the drawing, the King explains, in his fine yet idiosyncratic command of English, the details of the elephant's capture in the wild and its journey to the capital. 'The blessing curious she Elephant, of which the representation of likeness annexed herewith, was apprehended at the jungle of Radee in Eastern province of the Laos city named Yasodhon.... and has been remained at Yasodhon 9 months during the rainy season, and was conveyed from thence on February 1855, and safely arrived at Bangkok on 8th March 1855.'

Elephants with special characteristics such as light pigmentation were vital symbols of royal power and prosperity in old Thailand and were captured to be kept at court in royal splendour. These included the so-called 'white' elephants which were in fact a mottled light pink colour rather than actually white.

27 The Children of King Mongkut, *c.*1867–8.

Photographs, 5 × 9 cm.

Private Collection, London.

In these rare photographs dating from about the time of King Mongkut's death in 1868, about half of his 80 children are assembled, mainly younger ones. The photographs are in the popular carte-de-visite size first introduced in Paris in about 1860.

In 1868 King Mongkut's children aged between eight and eleven years of age numbered 25, and another twenty children were aged between two and seven. Many of them would have been the students of Mrs Anna Leonowens who taught in the palace school during the 1860s. Anna Leonowens became world famous in the Broadway musical 'The King and I' which largely misrepresented King Mongkut and his court.

Some of the princes who were to become prominent leaders in the reforms during the reign of King Chulalongkorn are probably included in this photograph, such as Prince Damrong who was born in 1862. The three Queens of King Chulalongkorn, the daughters of King Mongkut and Queen Piyamavadi (and therefore his half-sisters) were born in 1860, 1862, and 1864.

28 King Chulalongkorn (1853–1910) and Queen Sri Sawarinthira (1862–1955).

Two photographs, c.1885 22 × 28 and 21 × 27 cm.

British Library, Oriental and India Office Collections, Curzon Collection, Mss. Eur. F/111/ 88–89.

King Chulalongkorn's far-sighted reforms brought Siam into the modern world, and he steered a way through the crucial period of colonial expansion on the part of Britain and France. A number of border territories were lost in the process but the country survived.

Queen Sri Sawarinthira, also known as Queen Sawang Watthana, was the mother of Crown Prince Vajirunhis, and also of Prince Mahidol, founder of Thailand's first medical college, and father of the present King Bhumibol, as well as of six other princes and princesses. She gave birth to the Crown Prince when she was only fourteen, and lived to the age of 93, when she was the oldest Queen in modern history.

**29 Investiture of Crown Prince Maha Vajirunhis
(1878–1895).**

Photograph, 1887.

British Library, Oriental and India Office Collections, Curzon Collection,
Mss. Eur. F/111/ 88–89. Photograph, 20 × 25 cm.

King Chulalongkorn's eldest son by Queen Sri Sawarinthira was called
Maha Vajirunhis. He was named Crown Prince when he was nine.
Up to this time there had been no official appointment of a successor
to the throne, which caused many deadly rivalries among the
numerous claimants in previous centuries. Crown Prince Vajirunhis
died in 1895 when he was only sixteen, and the succession then passed
to the next eldest prince of rank, who in 1910 ascended the throne as
King Vajiravudh.

30 Royal Funerals, 1888.

View of the funeral chariots at the wall of the Grand Palace.
British Library, Oriental and India Office Collections, Curzon Collection,
Mss. Eur. F/111/ 88–89. Photograph. 20 × 26 cm.

The death of three of the youngest and highest-ranking children of
King Chulalongkorn in the year 1887 caused great sorrow to the
Royal Family and the court. All three were children of Queen
Saowapha, who was the mother also of King Vajiravudh and King
Prajadhipok.

The cremation of the two young princes and princess was a great
event in February 1888. Elaborate wooden funeral chariots were
constructed in accord with Thai royal custom. The chariots are visible
here from some high vantage point east of the Grand Palace *en route*
to the Royal Cremation Ground (called *Phra Men* or *Sanam Luang*, in
Thai).[1]

Prince Sirirat Kakutphan was less than two when he died. The King
began the construction of Thailand's first hospital from the wood used
in these funerals, and gave the hospital the prince's name. Princess
Phahurat Manimai died in her eighth year, and the Phahurat Market
south of the Royal Palace bears her name. Prince Triphet died only
three months after his sister, at the age of six.

Although the King had scores of children by his 150 minor wives,
the only ones eligible for succession to the throne were the sons of his
queens, three of whom were full sisters, and daughters of King
Mongkut, and hence half-sisters to King Chulalongkorn.

[1] Mrs. Florence Caddy was in Bangkok at the time of the funeral and described it in
her book. See Caddy 1889.

31 Photographs of Angkor Wat, c.1895.

British Library, Oriental and India Office Collections, Mss. Eur. F/111/ 84.

From the end of the late eighteenth century until 1907 when it was ceded to France, the Angkor region of Cambodia was a territory belonging to Siam, and travellers requested permission from Bangkok to travel there and see the architectural marvels, which were first made known by Henri Mouhot. By the 1890s Angkor was famous, and numerous travellers were making the long, slow overland journey from Bangkok. These photographs belonged to George Curzon who travelled in Siam (and Cambodia) in 1892 just after he assisted Lord Salisbury at the Foreign Office. Curzon took a keen interest in Siamese affairs.

By the 1890s photographs of this type may have been produced commercially to sell to visitors. They show:
A. A group of musicians playing in front of Angkor Wat.
B. Buddha images c. twelfth-thirteenth century, lined up in the storage depot.
C. The interior of one of the long galleries at Angkor Wat, with the date 1890 written on one of the pillars.

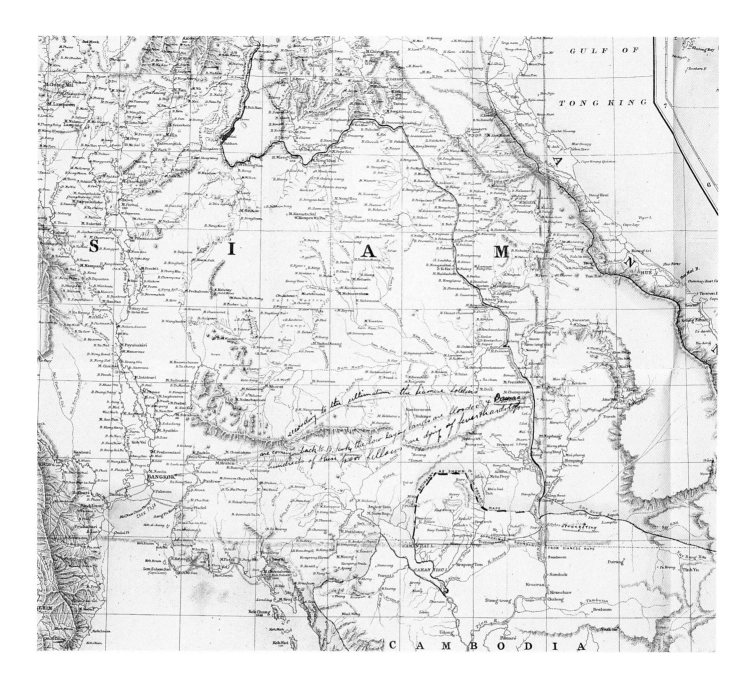

32 McCarthy's Map of Thailand, 1893.

British Library, Oriental and India Office Collections, Curzon Collection, Mss. Eur. F/111/87E, f.746.

Area shown, c.25 × 32 cm.

James McCarthy spent twelve years, from 1881 to 1893, compiling information for this complete map of Thailand on behalf of the Siamese Government Survey Department, of which he was the Director-General. He was given the Thai title of Phra Wiphak Phuwadon for his services.

In 1900 he published a detailed account of his experiences in travelling and collecting this information. A brief extract gives a sense of his long and arduous task:

'It was necessary to connect Sai with the triangulation which was being carried to Luang Prabang; but the haze was very thick, and even on favourable days a distance of about 4 miles was all that one could see. The time was occupied in cutting lines, and unsuccessful attempts were made for stars. One night, when the stars were twinkling feebly, I made an attempt to take observations; but there was a perfect plague of insects, which the men believed were spirits determined to prevent me from carrying on the work. I had a small hill cleared of jungle, and disclosed a pagoda, the existence of which had been unsuspected.'[1]

This copy of McCarthy's map belonged to George Curzon before he became Viceroy of India and was made Lord Curzon. Curzon was keenly interested in Siam, and followed affairs there with close attention. He has annotated his copy of the map, indicating the route taken by Thai soldiers in the year: 'according to the ultimatum the Siamese soldiers are coming back to B.kok, the low laying lands are flooded and hundreds of them poor fellows are dying of fever and hardship.'

[1] McCarthy 1900: 165.

THE LIFE OF THE BUDDHA

Thailand is widely known today for its fine Buddha images, most often made of bronze, and ranging in size from a few centimetres to many metres high. The images serve to remind us of the great life and teachings of the Buddha. The bronze images were modelled and cast in many styles over many centuries.

Similarly, the Buddha was widely represented in Thai painting by scenes of the events of his life, and of his previous lives, on the high interior walls of temples in dry fresco technique, and on large cloth banner paintings which were hung in temples. Less commonly, Thai manuscripts also depicted scenes of the Buddha's life, but scenes of his many previous lives were prevalent in illustrated manuscripts. These are the so- called birth tales of the Buddha. This contrasts with neighbouring Burma where the life of the Buddha was treated in great detail in manuscript painting. (see Herbert 1992)

The Ten Birth Tales (Thotsachat)

In Thailand it is the last ten of the nearly 550 tales of the previous lives of the Buddha before his birth as Prince Gautama that are depicted in paintings. The 550 tales are recorded in Buddhist scripture in the Pali language in a mixture of prose and verse. Illustrations of the ten last birth tales are more commonly found than ones illustrating the life of Prince Gautama, particularly in manuscript painting. Curiously, the illustrations never accompany the relevant scriptures that recount the birth tales. They are shown with extracts from the Abhidhamma section of Buddhist scripture, which treats psychological and philosophical subjects.

The very last of the ten birth tales was by far the most important. It was known as the Great Birth Tale (Mahachat), or else by its proper name, the Vessantara jataka, after the name of its hero, Prince Vessantara. Its narrative embodies the greatest of all Buddhist virtues, that of giving (dana in Pali). The retelling of the Great Birth tale was an act of Buddhist merit, and its recitation by monks was the occasion for a great celebration that lasted a full day and night. (See Anuman Rajadhon 1969)

The Vessantara tale

Prince Vessantara abandoned all his wealth and status. Giving away his sacred white elephant that assured good fortune in his kingdom, his people demanded that he be exiled. Vessantara led his wife and two children into the forest where they lived in poverty for seven months. Then he gave away his children to a disreputable old brahmin who mistreated them. Next he gave his wife Madri to the god Indra, disguised as a brahmin, but they were all protected by the gods and kept from harm, and finally reunited and installed in their kingdom.

Viewed superficially, the Vessantara story is difficult to understand, since the hero seems to needlessly inflict great pain on his beloved family. In fact it is a complex and deeply moving tale in which the desired goal of renunciation is achieved through the suffering caused to all the main characters.[1]

Traditionally paintings of the Vessantara tale were made in Thailand in large numbers. Long vertical cloth banners (called in Thai phrabot, meaning a cloth painting), usually on cotton, sometimes depicted key events in the Vessantara story. Very long horizontal cloth paintings called phaa phaweet (in northeastern dialect, meaning 'Vessantara cloth'), also on cotton with many scenes of the Vessantara tale, were used particularly in the northeast region, where they were hung up at temples, stretching many metres in length. (Gittinger 1992: 124–129)

Vessantara manuscripts recording the text of the story in Pali, and sometimes in Thai translation as well, were typically in the palm leaf format. They were frequently made as acts of merit, along with other Buddhist subjects, but when they were illustrated they were curiously not accompanied by illustrations from the story itself as we might expect. Instead they were often decorated with forest scenes and decorative motifs. As with the other birth tales, there was no specific correlation between the illustration and the texts. A small number of manuscript books contain only Vessantara illustrations (43).

---

[1] See Collins 1998: 497–554 for an analysis of Vessantara as an expression of the highest Buddhist felicity, and consequently for the relevance of the arcadian scenes found in the manuscripts.

33 Ten Birth Tales.

New York Public Library, Thai MS. 7.

Folding book manuscript of khoi paper, with 26 paired illustrations.
61.5 cm. wide.

Pali text (Abhidhamma extracts) in thick Cambodian script.

Like most Thai birth tale manuscripts, this one presents the ten stories
in paired illustrations on the left and right sides of the text, one pair
per tale. The text does not relate to the birth tales. Rather, it contains
extracts from the Abhidhamma section of Buddhist scriptures, which
treats psychological and philosophical subjects. This is true for all the
Thai manuscripts illustrating the birth tales.

Features such as the delicate, often pale background colours, with
an occasional solid red or orange background, the freedom and
large scale of the drawing, and the large flower motifs set in the
background, are all typical elements of earlier eighteenth century
Thai painting. The backgrounds are composed of simple landscape
elements, usually a flowering tree often with birds or some rockery,
but often rendered with great sophistication and delicacy. This
manuscript is a very fine example, probably of the early eighteenth

century, and is one of a small number of such Ayutthaya period
manuscripts to have survived. Scenes from two birth tales are seen
here. Above is the Temi birth tale, where the hero raises his chariot
before the astonished charioteer who has brought him, in an
apparently lifeless state, to be buried. In this tale the hero has
renounced all activity, knowing that harm will result from it.
Only when he is taken to be buried alive does he show his immense
strength. The composition, set on an orange ground, is brilliantly
vivid, with finely coloured detail. Below is the Mahajanaka birth tale,
in which a prince born in poverty returns to his native land to assume
his rightful place after a dramatic rescue from a shipwreck. The text
accompanying these illustrations begins 'kusala dhamma', opening
the Dhammasangini scripture.

Another example comes from the Bhuridatta tale, which exemplifies
the virtue of forbearance (p. 56–7). The hero is a serpent king (naga)
captured by an evil man to perform in public. The scene of the
capture, with the hero meditating while coiled round an anthill, is
bold in scale and colour, with large floral motifs, some sprouting from
behind the anthill and others hanging like garlands on the pink background. To the right, the evil captors are set in large scale against a

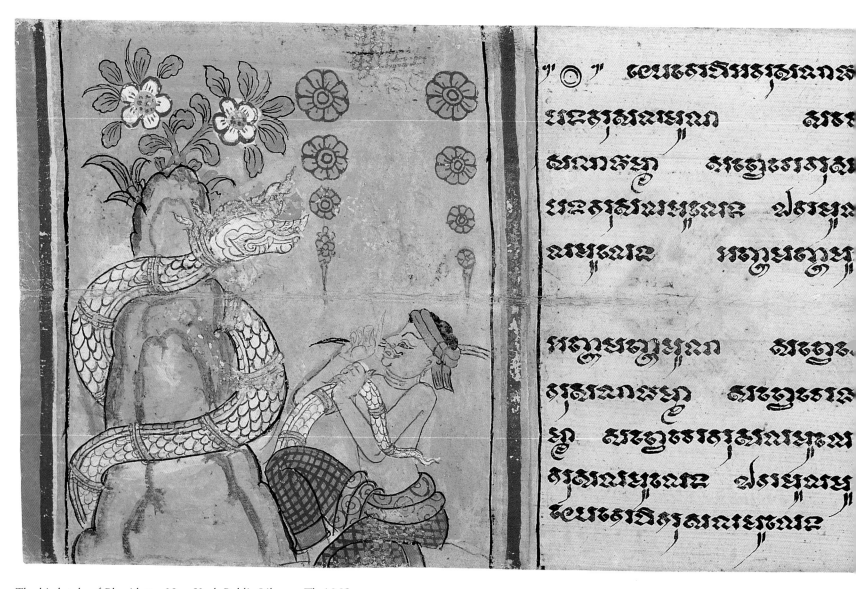

The birth tale of Bhuridatta. New York Public Library, Thai MS 7.

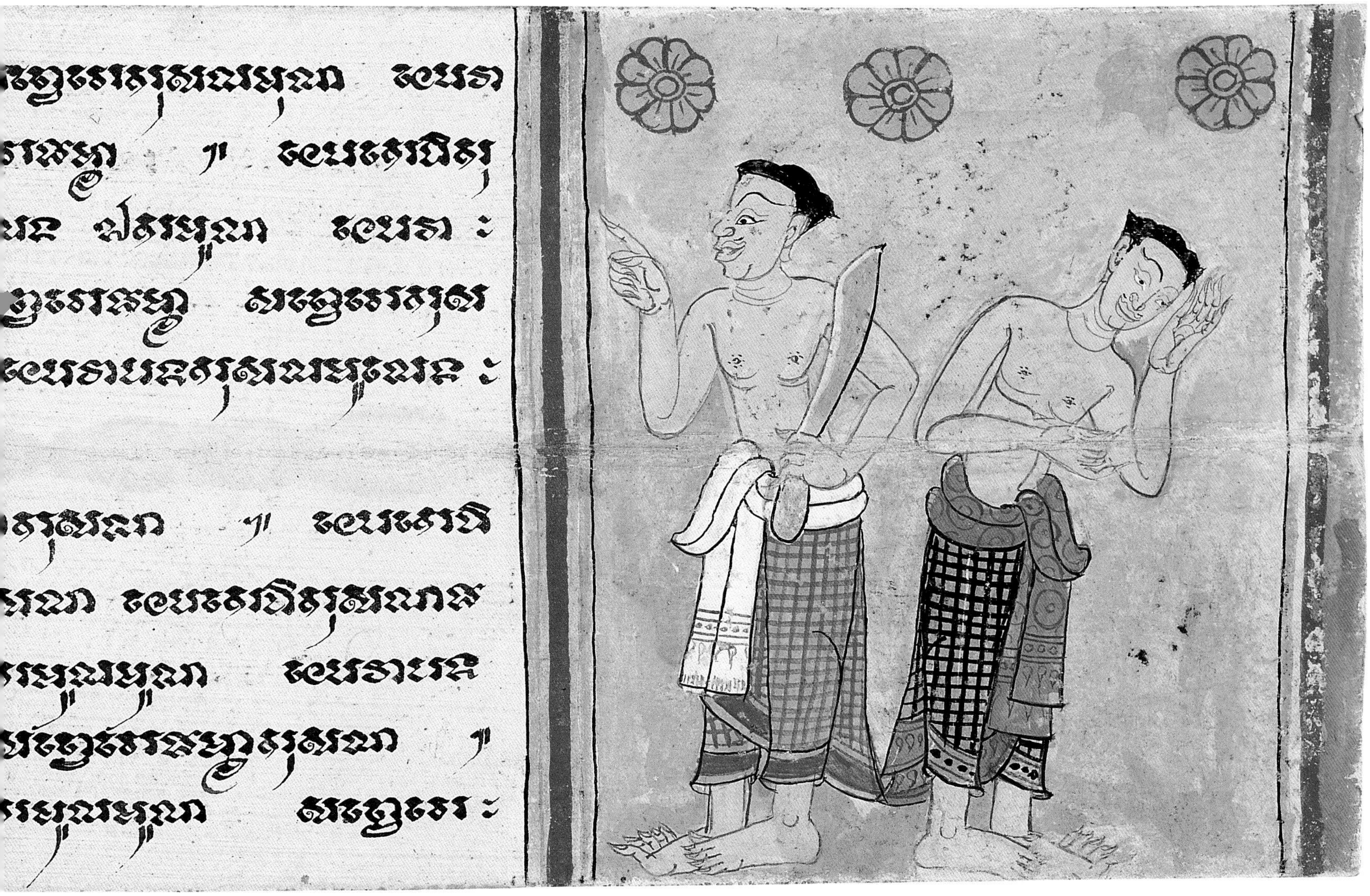

Scene in the Himavanta forests. New York Public Library, Thai MS 7.

plain background. Thai birth tale manuscripts of the Ayutthaya period very often include scenes of nature in the magic Himavanta forests which according to Buddhist cosmology are situated below the central cosmic mountain at the centre of the world. The forests constitute a land between earth and heaven which ordinary mortals cannot reach, a perfect world that is free of problems and suffering. The inhabitants of the forests are beings such as hermits who have attained magic powers through meditation, elephants and other real animals, and wondrous animals combining parts of different species, such as the *kinnara* (half-bird, half- human) and the *gajasingha* (half-lion, half-elephant). The inclusion of these magic forest scenes in Thai manuscript painting seems to cease in the late eighteenth century. The text here is from the Buddhist scripture entitled Kathavatthu.[1]

[1] For other paintings from this manuscript see Ginsburg 1989: 62, 70.

34 Ten Birth Tales of the Buddha.

New York Public Library, Thai MS. 6.

Folding book manuscript of khoi paper, with 28 paired illustrations. 62 cm wide.

Pali text (extracts from Abhidhamma scriptures) in thick Cambodian script.

This fine manuscript illustrating the Birth Tales is close in format and content to the previous one (33), though probably later in date, perhaps of the last quarter of the eighteenth century. In some respects it is also quite distinct, in its tighter, more restrained, composition and figure drawing, but the pale backgrounds, dimensions, and thick decorative script all suggest that it is still very much an Ayutthaya-period manuscript in type.

The artist has a personal way of depicting the Chinese-style hollow rockery, with high rising sweeps. Below, graceful kinnara couples disport themselves in idyllic settings. On the left (pp. 60–1) we find the most popular scene from the Vidhura tale, where the demon Punnaka flies on his magic horse through the skies hoping to destroy the hero Vidhura who must hold on for dear life to the horse's tail. Due to the hero's great merit, although in mortal danger he appears entirely calm and unconcerned.

In the scene from the Vessantara tale on the right, the hero gives away his sacred white elephant to the brahmins encountered on an excursion with his courtiers. He holds a golden water vessel, since the pouring of water symbolizes the gift. The text on this page is from the Dhammasangini scripture.[1]

From the latter section of the manuscript illustrating scenes in the magic Himavanta forest (p. 62), above, the magic wishing tree is ripe with maidens ready to pluck, and approached by a hermit and a deva. In the Buddhist texts the maidens, once picked, dissolve into nothingness, but the Thai pictorial imagination prefers a more concrete imagery. Below, a handsome kinnara couple embrace in a rocky forest setting.

[1] For another birth tale scene from this manuscript see Ginsburg 1989: 60.

The Vidhura and Vessantara birth tales. New York Public Library, Thai MS 6.

The magic wishing tree in the Himavanta forest, and a pair of Kinnaras. New York Public Library, Thai MS 6.

35 Ten Birth Tales of the Buddha.

British Library, Oriental and India Office Collections, India Office MS. Pali 207.

Folding book manuscript of khoi paper, with 30 paired illustrations. 60 cm wide.

Text in Pali (extracts from Abhidhamma scriptures) written in thick Cambodian script in black ink. Late eighteenth century.

Given to the India Office in 1825, this is perhaps the earliest acquired illustrated Thai manuscript in a British collection. A note at the end of the manuscript states that it was 'Presented by Ltt Coll Clifford by the hands of W Wigram Esqe, 9th Dec 1825'. Interestingly it came to Britain from Burma rather than from Thailand.[1]

The first twenty paired paintings illustrate the ten birth tales. Additional scenes follow them depicting the gods Indra and Brahma, angels, benevolent demons, and four informal scenes of monks with laymen, as often found in Phra Malai manuscripts. There is no Phra Malai text in this manuscript, only the typical extracts in Pali from the scriptures. The overall title of Mahabuddhaguna (Great Qualities of the Buddha) is given to the text.

The paintings are simply composed, but the artist's command of line and form, composition and colour, are all exemplary. The pale coloured backgrounds are typical of the late Ayutthaya and Thonburi periods.

In the Bhuridatta birth tale the Buddha to be is born as a great serpent (or naga) who exemplifies the virtue of forebearance. He is captured by evil men who obtain a magic spell. They torment the serpent and force him to perform. On the left, coiled round his ant hill where he fasts and meditates, the hero is shown during his capture. His captor holds a small branch to sprinkle the hero with water containing the spell, thus subduing him. To the right, in a scene which precedes the capture, the naga hero is attended by naga maidens dancing before him. A small bird adorns each of the paintings, typical of the Thai artist's keen observation of natural life. The text here is the Vibhanga scripture from the Abhidhamma.

In the Candakumara birth tale (p. 64), a ceremony is plotted by evil brahmins to sacrifice the Buddha to be, but the god Indra descends from heaven and destroys the ceremony and the evil brahmins. The group of animals on the left are part of the sacrifice and include an elephant as small as the horse and goat. The text begins the extracts from the Kathavatthu scripture.

The last pair of scenes from this manuscript depict monks and laymen in the way they are frequently shown in Phra Malai manuscripts, engaged in drinking tea and play. The monks on the left are neglecting their serious pursuits, seated before a floral curtain, with a board game and spittoon, while on the right the local people prepare tea and sweets for them. The Pali text ends here with the title Mahabuddhaguna (Great Qualities of the Buddha).

[1] Lt. Col. Miller Clifford, served in the British Army during a long career beginning in the West Indies in 1794. In 1824 he was with the 89th Regiment of Foot in the first Burma war, which was where he must have acquired this fine Thai manuscript. Wigram was a director of the East India Company; he doubtless carried the manuscript to England on Clifford's behalf.

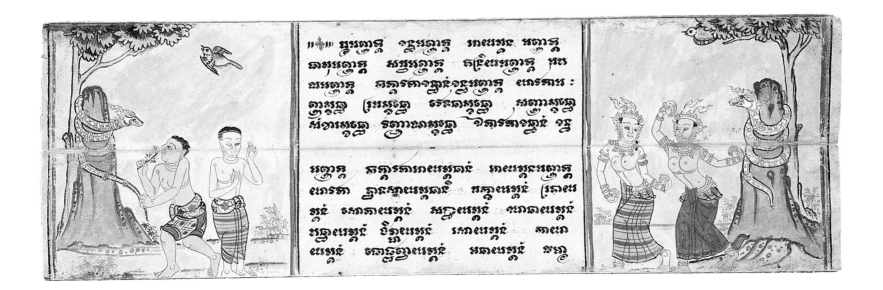

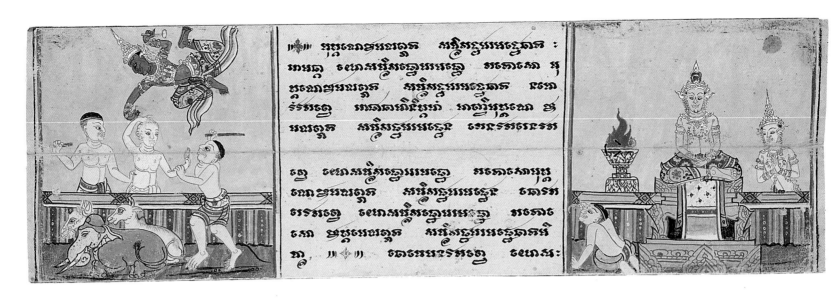

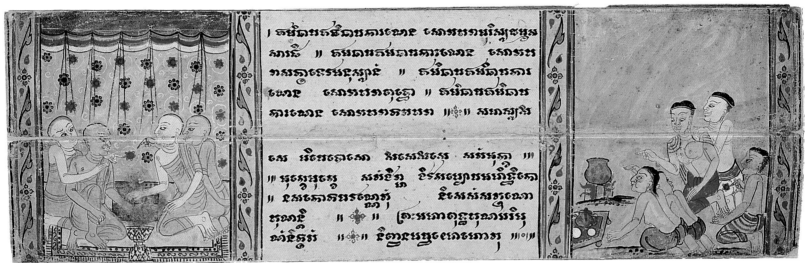

Candakumara birth tale (*above*), and genre scene of monks. British Library, India Office MS Pali 207.

36 Life of the Buddha & Ten Birth Tales.

Bodleian Library, Oxford. MS. Pali a.27.
Folding book manuscript of khoi paper, with 40 paired paintings.
66.5 cm. wide.
Lacquer and gilt covers with lozenge design.
Pali text (extracts from the Buddhist canon) written in thick Cambodian script.

The discovery of this richly illustrated Thai manuscript, with eighteen paired scenes depicting the Buddha's life, and a further 22 scenes of the Ten Birth Tales, was momentous .[1] Manuscripts illustrating the events from the life of the Buddha are rare in Thailand.

Housed in the Pali manuscript collection of the Bodleian Library since 1819, when a Mr W. C. Gibson deposited it there, it was not recognized as a Thai manuscript. In fact it had travelled to England not from Thailand, but from Srilanka. How it had originally reached Srilanka from Thailand is not known. A note in English attached to the manuscript by Mr B. Clough of Ceylon and dated 1819 explains that it came from a temple in Kandy.[2]

The text is almost entirely in the Pali language, containing the usual excerpts from Abhidhamma scriptures. It is written in the thick Cambodian script typical of the Ayutthaya period, with only a few words of text in the Thai language.

The painting in this manuscript is close enough to the 1776 Traiphum manuscripts and the 1780 manuscript in the Chester Beatty Library (37, see p. 72) to suggest it was made at about the same time. The figure types are similar in their scale, details and dress. However the backgrounds are solid bright colours, red or yellow, and also blue and green, whereas the dated examples use pale colour grounds for the most part. The bright ground colours are generally seen to be characteristic of late eighteenth-century painting, and may have been an innovation at this time. Further evidence will hopefully help us define these changes in Thai painting style.

Four scenes (on pp. 66–7) show: the Multiplication of the Buddha's image against flames and a bodhi tree (upper left), the offering of a mango by Sujata (upper right), the Buddha enthroned in Tusita heaven above the three headed elephant of the god Indra (lower left), and the descent from Tusita heaven (lower right). The compositions are dense, but clearly and simply organized. Depth is limited to a foreground that meets the sky or a tall hill of rock.

Further scenes (pp. 68–9) show Prince Gautama cutting his hair as he begins his search for enlightenment (left), and later (on the right) lying on an elaborate couch after his austerities, with Indra demonstrating the three strings of the lute that indicate the middle way, or the way of moderation. Below, an offering to the Buddha, and to the right, the Buddha's victory over the forces of evil and illusion in the form of an army of demons. The paintings are richly coloured and detailed. In the hair cutting, the figures of grieving horse and groom are very close to those in the 1780 manuscript in Dublin (37). The Pali text here is titled Sahassanaya, a frequent term for the Buddhist canonical extracts.

On pp. 70–1 Prince Vessantara, seated in his elegant hermitage set in the rocky hill behind it, with his wife Madri respectfully at his side, is about to give her away to a poor brahmin who is actually the god Indra in disguise. Vessantara will pour water from his water vessel to symbolize the gift. The brahmin's body is green (Indra's own colour), and the god also appears above him hovering in the sky, observing the scene. Above right we witness the gift of the prince's two children to the brahmin Jujaka, a comical and unattractive character. Simultaneously we see in the same frame their mother Madri wandering in the forest, confronted by the (harmless) wild animals who are sent by the gods to prevent her returning too soon to the hermitage while the children are being given to Jujaka. Below are early scenes of the life of Prince Gotama, first, his birth in the grove called Lumbini, attended by the gods (on the left). The golden infant, in a standing posture and pointing, is held in one of the four hands of the god Brahma. To the right is depicted the encounter of the young prince with the Four Signs or Omens, an old man, a sick man, a corpse, and a monk, which first sets him on the course of escaping the world and seeking enlightenment.

[1] For the discovery of the manuscript we are indebted to the Pali scholar Mme J Filliozat. Thai temple murals nearly always illustrated the life of the Buddha. In neighbouring Burma the Buddha's life was illustrated in great detail in manuscript painting, but not in Thailand. See Herbert 1992.

[2] The Rev. Benjamin Clough of the Wesleyan mission in Ceylon published a Sinhalese English Dictionary (1821–30), a grammar of the Pali language (1824) and a translation of the ritual of Buddhist monks (Kammavaca) in 1831.

Scenes from the life of the Buddha. Bodleian Library, Oxford. MS. Pali. a. 27.

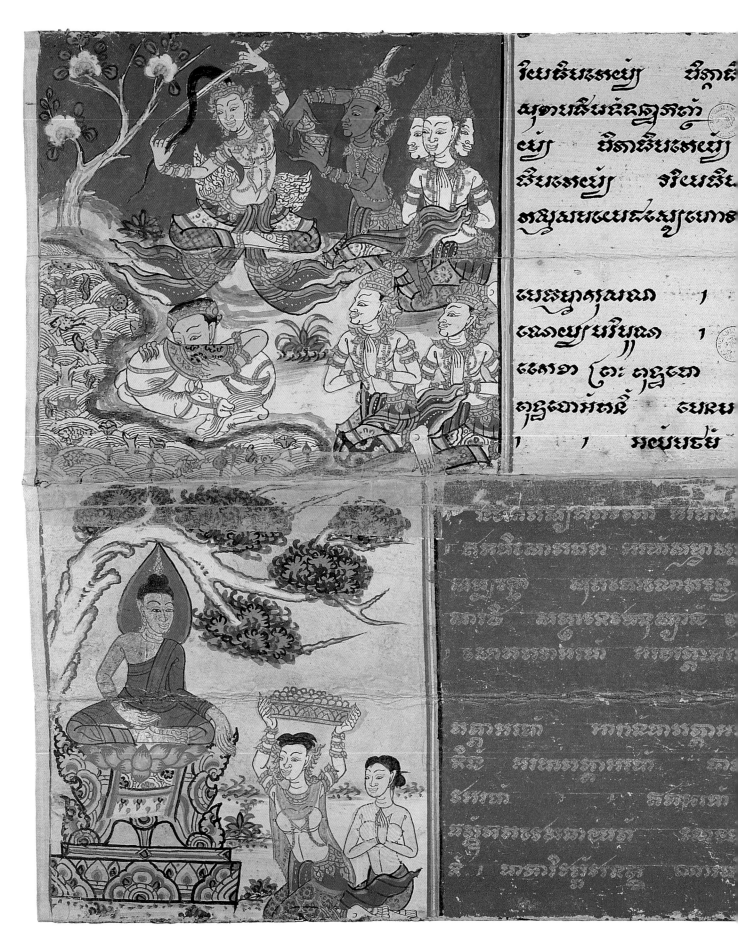

Scenes of the Buddha's life. Bodleian Library, Oxford. MS. Pali. a. 27.

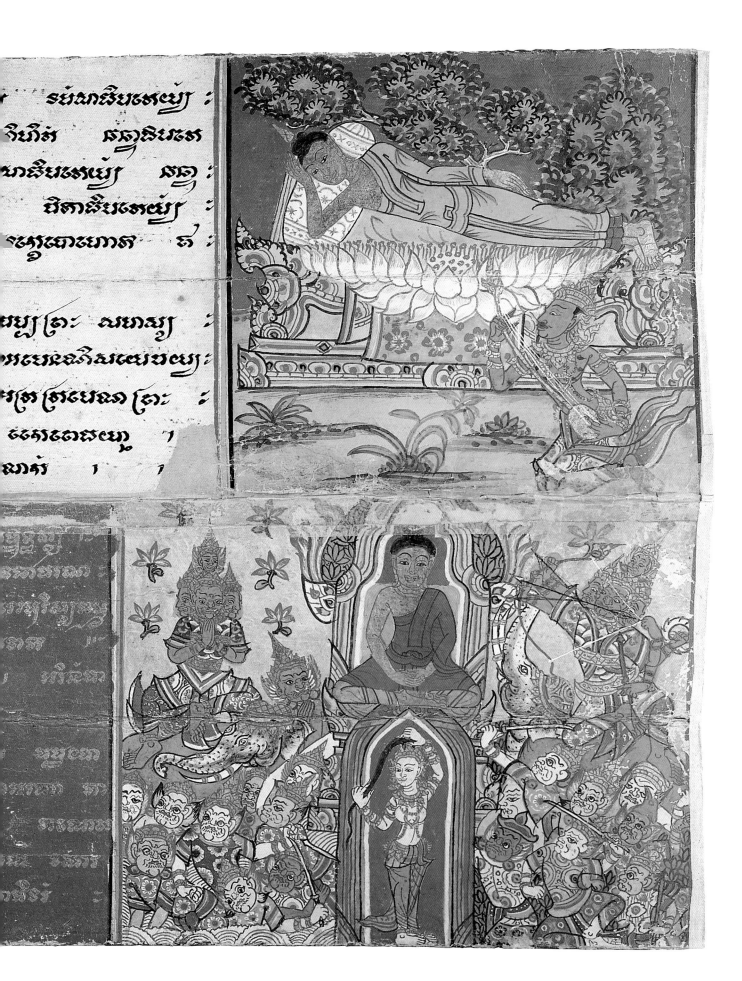

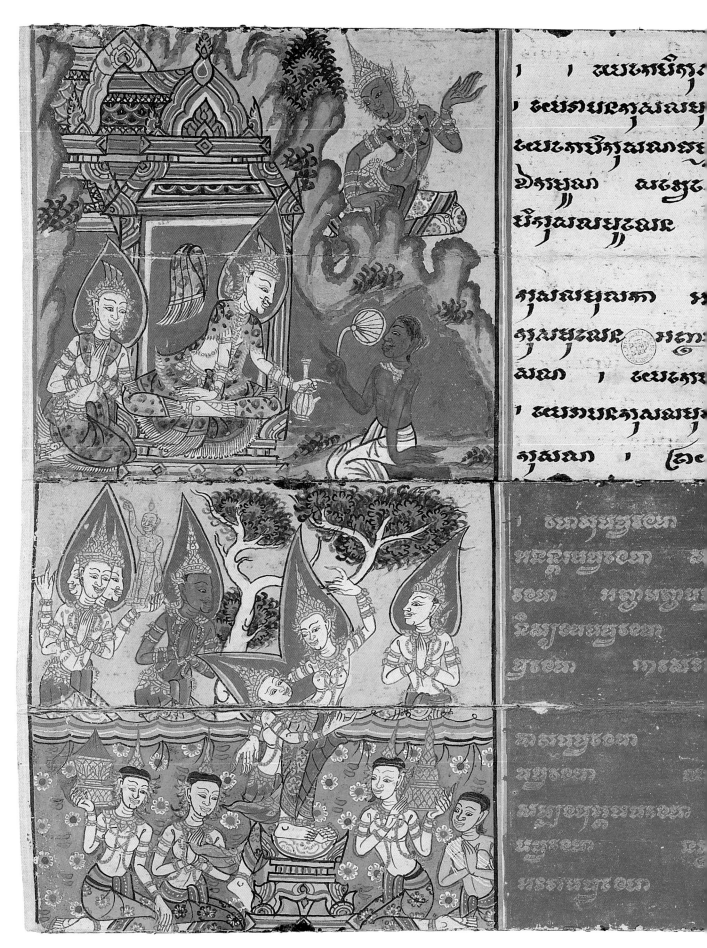

The birth tale of Vessantara (*above*), and scenes from the life of the Buddha (*below*). Bodleian Library, Oxford. MS. Pali. a. 27.

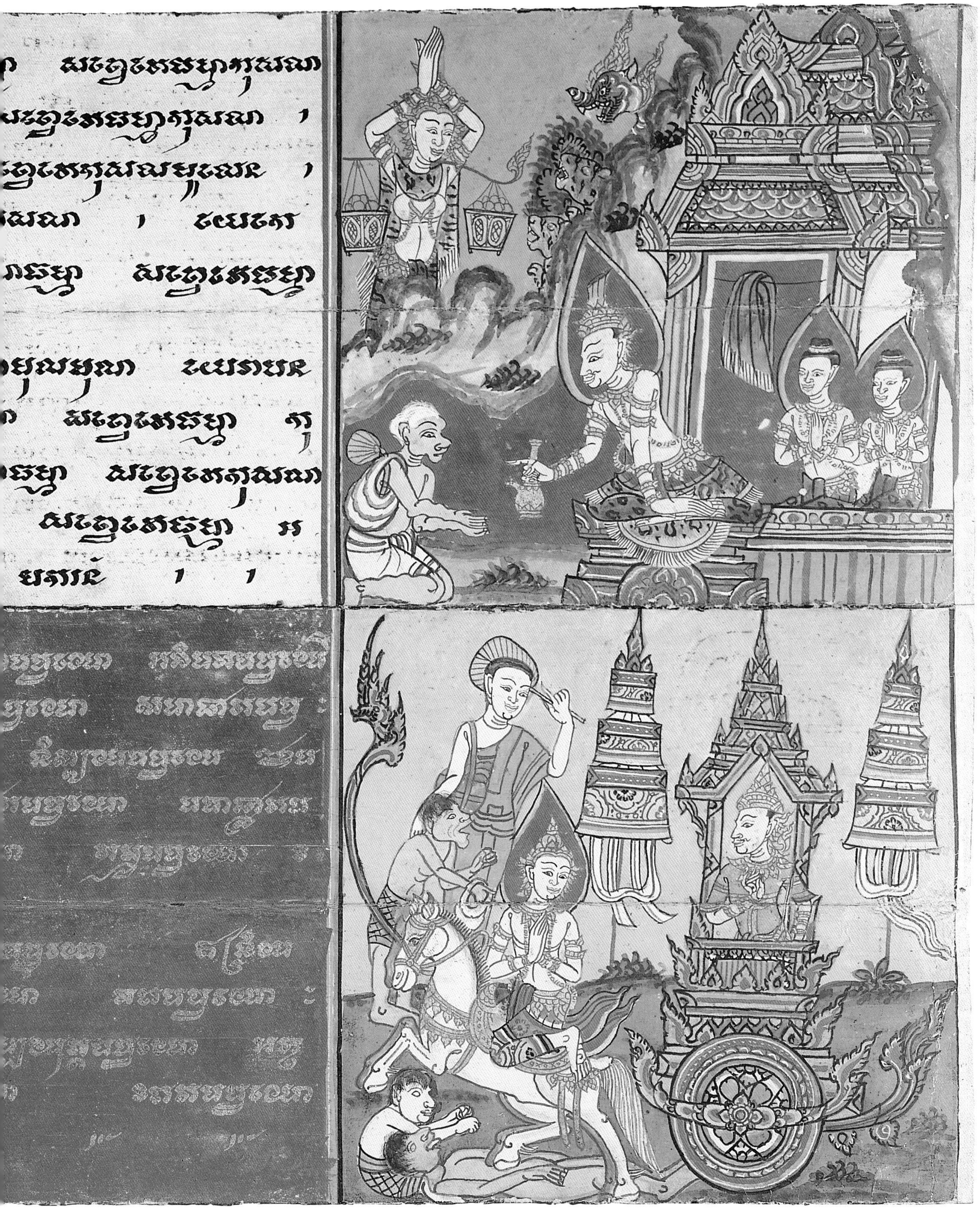

37 Ten Birth Tales, with scenes from the Buddha's Life, dated 1780.

Chester Beatty Library, Dublin, Thai MS. 1340.

Folding book manuscript of khoi paper, with 30 paired illustrations. 62 cm wide.

Pali text (extracts from Abhidhamma scriptures) written in thick Cambodian script.

The date in the colophon in this manuscript is equivalent to 1780 AD. The year is given in two calendar cycles, the year of the Rat in the twelve year cycle, and year two of the ten year cycle, a combination which recurs only every 60 years. It says that the manuscript was completed on the third day of the week on the eleventh day of the waxing moon, which was on October 1 1780. The scribe also gives his name, Chui.

The date makes this manuscript a valuable landmark in the development of Thai painting style. It is in fact quite close stylistically to the two Traiphum manuscripts that are dated to the year 1776 so three illustrated manuscripts now can be firmly placed in the Thonburi period (1767–1781) when Siam was recovering from the destruction of the old capital at Ayutthaya.[1]

The Ten birth tales are represented with a pair of scenes from each tale. Two events from the Buddha's life are also depicted, the cutting of Gautama's hair, with his grieving horse and charioteer, and another with ladies making an offering.

Here we see the birth tales of Janaka (above) and Sama, where the demon king misguidedly kills the hero when he fetches water for his blind parents. The last pair of scenes represent Nimi's visit to hell.

The style of this manuscript continues the traditions of Ayutthaya painting, with pale ground colours and decorative flora in quite simple settings. The dramatic dark background that will often characterize painting of the early Bangkok period is not yet found here.

The overall title of Mahabuddhaguna is given to the texts, as was common.

[1] See Wenk 1965 for the 1776 manuscript in Berlin, and *Buddhist Cosmology Thonburi Version* 1982 for the one in Bangkok.

38 Ten Birth Tales of the Buddha.

British Library, Oriental and India Office Collections. Or. 14526.

Folding book manuscript, incomplete, of khoi paper, with eight paired paintings surviving. 60 cm wide.

Pali text (Abhidhamma extracts) and Thai commentary, written in thin Cambodian script.

The artist has filled the spaces beside the text area, that are usually separated by borders, with large-scale figures, rendered with great vitality and freedom of line. There is no background colouring and no borders for the painting. Only four of the ten birth tale illustrations survive in this fragmentary manuscript, plus an illustration of two seated ladies.

We see here the Sama birth tale, which exemplifies the virtue of devoted service. On the right, the demon king Piliyakkha is misguidedly about to kill the hero, Sama. The king is full of energy, in the characteristic posture which derives from Thai dance. His fatal arrow will fly directly across the text itself unimpeded by any dividing borders. The gentle hero, Sama, stands with his water bag, intended for the succour of his blind parents, balanced on the back of a friendly deer, and he seems blissfully unaware of his impending death. The same treatment is afforded to the Bhuridatta tale, isolating the main characters, with the hero on the left, meditating while coiled round the ant hill and the grotesque and comical villain on the right, about to capture him.

The intermediate dimensions of the manuscript, the height measurement of 13 cm. falling between the typical Ayutthaya examples (9–11 cm. high) and the larger nineteenth century ones (c. 14 cm.) further support a date in the late eighteenth century, as does the use of the thin form of Cambodian script. There is an incomplete dated colophon, giving the day and month, but not the year. It mentions the sponsor, Khrua Rak of Wat Prasat, and the scribe's name, sami (for samian?) Ratanachot. The Wat Prasat temple may be one of that name in Phetburi, and in fact the plain backgrounds are a notable feature of Phetburi school painting. Some of the text is in the Thai language, being a commentary on Buddhist subjects, but on the page shown here the text is in Pali and begins: parihana dhammo aparihana dhammo.

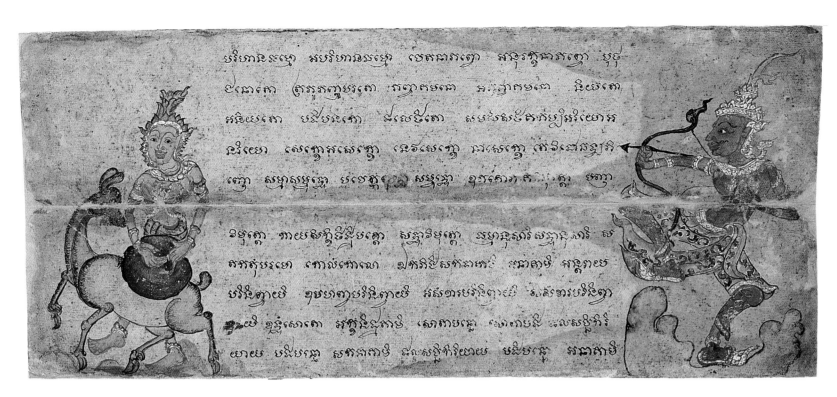

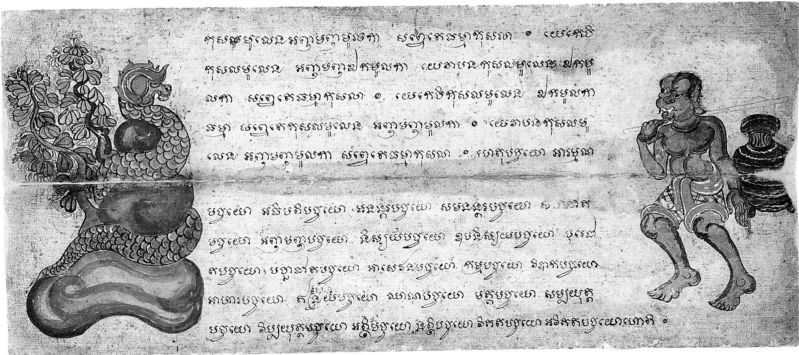

The shooting of Sama by the misguided demon king (*above*).
Bhuridatta's imminent capture by the evil brahmin (*below*).
British Library, Or. 14526.

The capture of Bhuridatta (*left*) and the death of Sama (*right*).

39 Ten Birth Tales.

British Library, Oriental and India Office Collections. Or. 14704.

Folding book manuscript of khoi paper, with twelve paired illustrations. 61.5 × 12.5 cm. (Cover folds lacking.) Pali text of Abhidhamma extracts, and Thai text of the Phra Malai story, written in thin Cambodian script.

Although considerably worn and rubbed, this fine manuscript depicted the Ten Birth tales with an elegant and vigorous drawing style and refined colour sense. It can probably be attributed to the last decade of the eighteenth century, based in part on similarities with the example of 1797 (see pp. 78–79). Its figures are large in scale, and background colours are often dark, characteristics of the early Bangkok period. The combination of the birth tale illustrations with the text of the Phra Malai story is also typical at this time. The

geometric border designs with long diamond lozenge shapes relate to some of the borders in the 1797 manuscript.

In the tale of Bhuridatta we find the scene of the hero as a serpent king under attack by the evil brahmin sprinkling him with drops of magic water to subdue him. Foliage and flowers are rendered in a schematic way, and the colouring subtly contrasts the pink background with the steel grey of the ant hill.

The same elements bring the Sama tale to life, with the stricken hero, attended by two large-scale deer, and the demon king, opposite, filling the entire frame with the graceful posture deriving from Thai dance.

Opposite. The misguided demon king loosing the fatal arrow.

40 Ten Lives of the Buddha and Phra Malai, dated 1797.

Chester Beatty Library (Dublin). Thai MS. 1310.

Folding book manuscript of khoi paper, 64 cm. wide. Red lacquer covers. 24 paired illustrations.

Pali text (extracts from the Buddhist canon) followed by Thai text of the Phra Malai legend, in thin Cambodian script.

The colophon of this manuscript dates it to year of the horse, 2340 in the Buddhist era, corresponding to 1797 AD, and makes this a major document in tracing the painting styles of the early Bangkok period. The sombre and often dramatic background colours of this manuscript are in dark blue and other dark shades, alternating with orange and pink grounds. They represent a clear change in taste from the bright red and yellow grounds or pale colours that were prevalent in earlier decades.

In the shipwreck scene from the Janaka tale (right) the turbulent sea stretches to the top of the painting, and the goddess descending to rescue the hero, surrounded by a rich red aureole with a curling edge, is viewed as if from above. The artist has eloquently rendered the excitement of the wreck, although he omits the ship which is usually included. On the left the goddess sails through the air carrying the hero to safety, against a dark blue ground.

In the Sama tale the misguided demon King (right) lets fly his arrow which kills the hero who stands with a friendly deer (left), while his water pot, of red earthenware, spills and falls, all set against a plum-coloured background. The deer is particularly appealing with its elongated head and neck. The delicate, feathery details of plants and foliage set off the figures. The settings are simple, usually with a single decorative motif balancing the figures. There is no attempt to show distance, or to clearly identify a ground space. The varying geometric borders are also distinctive, though they may continue earlier conventions.

The text on these pages quotes from the Pali Vibhanga text in the Abhidhamma scripture. The script is Cambodian, but not of the thick type popular in the earlier period. In fact the thick decorative script seems to be little employed after the late eighteenth century, and the use of the thin script may itself indicate a date later than the 1780s.

The text of the Phra Malai tale is included in this manuscript, even though the Phra Malai story is not illustrated. The combination of Phra Malai text with the birth tale paintings was becoming common in the early Bangkok period. Later on, the paintings came to illustrate the Phra Malai story almost exclusively.

41 Ten Lives of the Buddha and Phra Malai, dated 1813.

Honolulu Academy of Art, 2961–1.

Folding book manuscript of khoi paper, with 26 paired paintings. 66 cm. wide.

Text in Thai and Pali written in thin Cambodian script, and also some Thai script.

According to its colophon this elegant manuscript was made in the year 2356 of the Buddhist era, equivalent to 1813 AD. Its date provides us with another valuable benchmark in the development of Thai manuscript painting. As with the 1797 manuscript (above), the text is that of the Phra Malai tale, written in Thai language but using the Cambodian script. Here, however, the Ten Birth tales and the Phra Malai story are both illustrated. Twelve of the 26 paired illustrations depict the Phra Malai story.

At the beginning of the text are the familiar Abhidhamma extracts in the Pali language, each identified with its title in Thai script rather than the Cambodian script of the main text. Atypically the ten birth tales are represented by single scenes rather than by a pair of scenes for each tale. Hence four tales appear on two of the first folds, that of Temi (upper left), Janaka (upper right), Bhuridatta (lower left) and Mohosadha (lower right). (p. 80–1)

Background colours are consistently dark in tone, as we have noticed in manuscripts made in the early Bangkok period.

The artist is suave and sophisticated in his compositions, which are rather bold and large scale.

42 Vessantara Illustrations.

Vessantara scenes. Painting on cotton cloth. North Thailand (Lanna), nineteenth century.

British Museum, Department of Oriental Antiquities, 1926. 2–17.03 and 04. 79 × 100 cm.

A northern Thai painting on cloth from a set represents the Vessantara tale in a distinctly northern style. Above, Prince Vessantara pours water from a vessel down to a group of eight rowdy brahmins. The pouring of water is a symbolic gesture that indicates a gift, so it represents the giving of the elephant to the brahmins who have asked for it. The noble prince is at the centre of the painting, attended by a servant bearing the royal umbrella indicating his rank. Next to him a brief text labels the scene in the script of northern Thailand-'Vessantara gives away his white elephant'. To the right, an elegant structure represents the world of luxury and its occupations which Vessantara will abandon. People are shown in it, busy with their daily lives. To the left the raucous brahmins make a strong contrast, set against a hill wild with monkeys in trees above. The style of painting is typically northern. The outlines are soft, and tempered by shading. The colouring is pale, compared to the vivid colours of central Thai painting.

Four birth tales, dated 1813.
Honolulu Academy of Art,
2961–1.

Vessantara gives away his white elephant. Painting on cotton cloth, north Thailand, nineteenth century.
(British Museum, Department of Oriental Antiquities.)

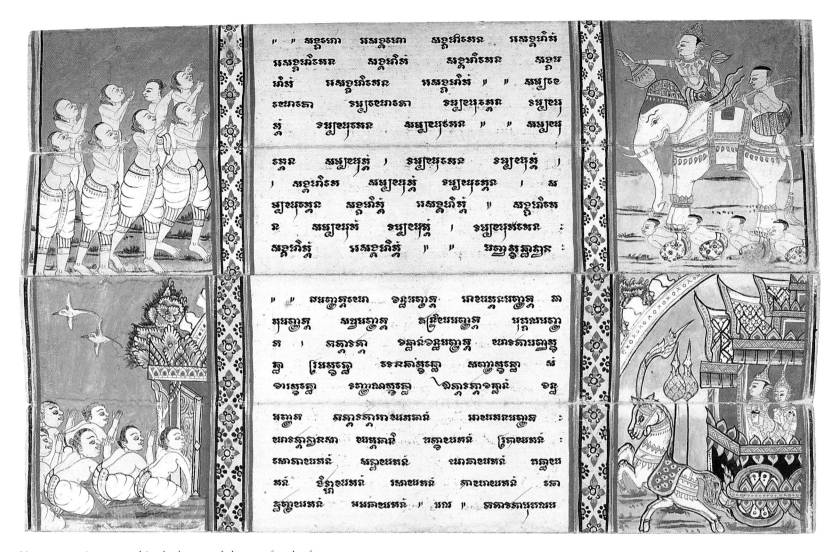

Vessantara gives away his elephant and departs for the forest.

43 The Vessantara Birth tale (the Great Birth tale).

Chester Beatty Library, Dublin. Thai MS. 1341.

Folding book manuscript of khoi paper with fourteen paired illustrations. 61.5 cm. wide.

Pali text in thick Cambodian script.

Manuscripts that specifically illustrate the Vessantara tale are unusual in Thailand, although the story is in fact enormously important in Thai buddhism. One or two scenes from the Vessantara story are of course allotted in the illustrated series of Ten birth tales. This manuscript, however fully depicts the tale in fourteen scenes.

The text is in the Pali language and contains not the text of the Vessantara story itself but extracts of the seven usual Pali texts.

The gift of the royal elephant to the eight brahmins is depicted on p. 83, with the brahmins on the left and the prince pouring water from his seat on the elephant's back, symbolizing the gift. The pair of scenes below these depict the departure of Vessantara and his family for the forest in their chariot. The border patterns and colours vary on each illustrated page, and relate closely to Thai patterns on contemporary

textiles. (Guy 1998: 121–151). The manuscript probably dates from the late eighteenth century.

Two details (above) show the family's rather palatial hermitage, appropriate to the great merit of the hero, and set in strange mushroom-like rockery. Above, Chuchok handles a red implement at the side of the hermitage, and below Vessantara gives his wife Madri to the disguised god Indra who has come to request her in order to be able to protect her. Although disguised, his green body indicates his identity.

Actual texts of the Vessantara story in old Thailand were frequent, some in Pali and others in Thai language. Curiously the texts are illustrated not with the story itself, but with scenes of the magical Himavanta forests that lie between the human world and the cosmic mountain at the center of the world. The association of this story with idealized scenery is entirely appropriate however, for the Vessantara story is a supreme expression of 'Buddhist felicities'. (Collins 1998: 497–554.) The idyllic forest scenes are similarly depicted in other Buddhist manuscripts we have surveyed.

BUDDHIST SUTRAS

Beside the main Buddhist subjects surveyed in this book – The ten Birth tales, Phra Malai and the Traiphum cosmology – other subjects served to illustrate Thai Buddhist texts. The creatures of the magical forest, frequently included in Ten Birth manuscripts, were sometimes themselves the main subject of illustration – the devas (minor divinities), hermits and ascetics who gained access to the magic forests by devout practices, and wondrous creatures half-human and half-animal such as kinnara (bird-human) and narasinha (lion-human). The 'magic forest' illustrations all seem to date from the eighteenth century, and we can suppose they were probably made before that as well. Fanciful figures such as foreigners – Persians, Europeans and Chinese – were also used for the decoration of these manuscripts. Other Buddhist texts however were adorned with decorative geometric or floral motifs alone.

By the early nineteenth century all these decorative elements accompanying Buddhist texts ceased to be popular, for some reason, and the transition seems to coincide with the growing production of Phra Malai manuscripts. But a new subject appeared as accompaniment to Buddhist texts, a series of seated Buddha images, often seven in number, attended by pairs of attendants, different in each of seven illustrations. The text in these manuscripts can be either the normal selection of Abhidhamma extracts in the Pali language, or else the Phra Malai text in Thai, with both texts written in the thin form of Cambodian script. The size of these manuscripts with seated Buddhas is markedly smaller than that of the Phra Malai books.

Another type, either new or continuing older traditions, illustrates Buddhist teachings through metaphorical images. Animal forms represent concepts such as greed, desire, and ignorance (see Buddhadasa 1969).

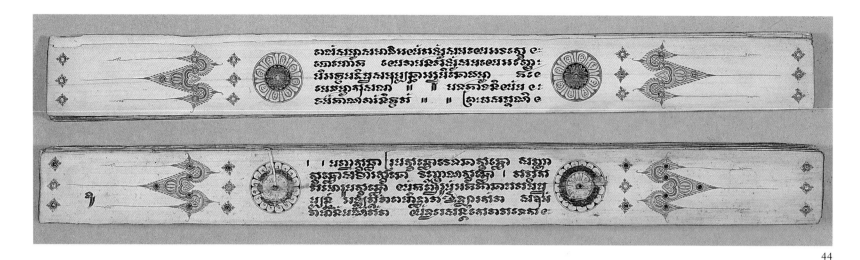

44

45

44 Buddhist Prayers (Texts from Abhidhamma scriptures).

Chester Beatty Library, Dublin. Thai MS. 1335.

Palm leaf manuscript. 55 cm. wide. Pali language text in thick Cambodian script.

The Pali text shown here is from the Dhammasangini section of the Abhidhamma scriptures, one of the seven texts usually quoted in illustrated Thai Buddhist manuscripts. It is written in the thick Cambodian script that was used for Buddhist texts until the late eighteenth century.

Embellished with curved and geometric forms, and with lotus blooms in the roundels, this manuscript most probably dates from the eighteenth century. It probably stands at the end of a long tradition of palm leaf decoration dating back for hundreds of years previously, although few examples of this abstract decoration have survived.

46

45 Buddhist Prayers (Texts from Abhidhamma scriptures).

Chester Beatty Library (Dublin). Thai MS. 1346.

Folding book manuscript, with geometric illustrations. 59.5 cm. wide. Pali language text in Cambodian script.

This folding book version of the Pali scriptural texts is another rare survival, with abstract decoration very similar to that in the last example. The folding book originally must have imitated the palm leaf manuscript in its shape and dimensions. We can only guess at what period the folding book first came into use in Thailand, for the oldest surviving ones are not earlier than the sixteenth or seventeenth century. The palm leaf manuscripts on the other hand are sure to have an older history, for they continue a type of palm leaf book well known from India and Nepal as far back as the tenth century and before. The long and thin pages of this folding book connect it visibly to the palm leaf format.

46 Buddhist Prayers (Texts from Abhidhamma scriptures).

Chester Beatty Library, Dublin. Thai MS. 1343.

Folding book manuscript. 63.5 cm. wide. Pali and Thai texts in thick and thin forms of Cambodian scripts.

The dimensions of the book, the uncoloured grounds for the painting, the light character of the draftsmanship, and the thick form of Cambodian script are all features characteristic of the end of the Ayutthaya period, so this manuscript may be provisionally dated to the third quarter of the eighteenth century.

The Pali Abhidhamma scriptures are adorned with isolated subjects, such as birds, devas, kinnaras (half-bird, half-humans), and a European and a Persian holding floral sprays, shown here. Just below them on a page without text the artist has depicted the forces of Mara assaulting Gautama's concentration during his search for enlightenment, and the flood waters loosed by the Earth Goddess to thwart them.

A colophon at the end of this text names the sponsor of the book as Mu'n Phrom. No date is given.

Seated monks (*top*).
Confronted lions (*above*) and Devas on thrones.

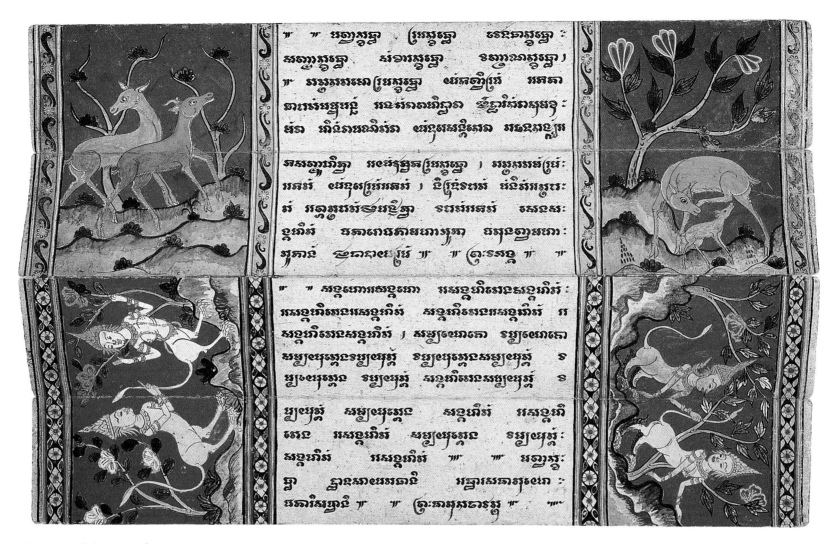

Creatures of the magic forests.

47 Buddhist Prayers (Texts from Abhidhamma scriptures).

Chester Beatty Library (Dublin). Thai MS. 1345.

Folding book manuscript, 58 cm. wide.
Pali language text, in Cambodian script.

The texts from Buddhist scripture are illustrated in this manuscript with a variety of decorative subjects including Chinese 'snow lions', other animals, and devas (minor divinities). They are set upon solid red backgrounds that are adorned with large white-outlined flowers. Monks are also depicted, with lively faces achieved through simple and sure calligraphic lines. Their hands and feet are expressively elongated.

Confronted lions, doubtless borrowed from Chinese sources, are adapted to the Thai context. Below them, elegant devas are seated on energetic thrones, the red ground behind them embellished with foliage outlined in white. Below them are tenderly depicted deer, and men with the bodies of animals, characteristic creatures of the magic Himavanta forests.

Each of the decorative border patterns is different. The text begins 'Itipiso bhagava...', indicating excerpts from the Vibhanga scripture.

48 Buddhist Prayers (Texts from Abhidhamma scriptures).

British Library, Oriental and India Office Collections, I.O. Pali 152.

Folding book of khoi paper, with eighteen paired illustrations. 62 cm. wide. Pali text in Cambodian script.

This unusual book offers a variety of forest scenes, including hunters, animal life, and devas to accompany the usual excerpts from Abhidhamma texts in Pali. The scenes are set on a background of abstract rockery that seems to be idiosyncratic to this artist. The colour choices are also different and unusual, with a palette mainly of green, plum, orange, yellow and brick red, as well as pink, and blue. The painting of this manuscript is unfinished, which provides us with insights into the methods used in making it. Its unfinished state might

also account for the unusual colour choices, as the final colours might have been different. Primary sketches for the paintings are visible in red.

In the two lower scenes illustrated, for example, the trees were apparently outlined first, and given an undercolour of pink (right) and yellow (left). The ground colour was also added at an early stage in a rust, and the green of the foliage was painted in. Further details have been added on the left to delineate the tree trunk and the leaves, while they are not yet present on the right. The last line of the text on this page gives the name Mahabuddhaguna (the Qualities of the Buddha) to the texts, a common appelation for the Abhidhamma excerpts.

Based on its general format, its dimensions with a relatively small height of 11 cm., and also on the use of the thick form of Cambodian script, the book may possibly date from 1760–80.

49 Buddhist Prayers and Phra Malai, dated 1880.

British Library, Oriental and India Office Collections, Or. 15246.

Folding book manuscript of khoi paper with eighteen paired illustrations. 36 × 12 cm. Pali and Thai text in Cambodian script.

Seven images of the Buddha are depicted in this book, all in the same seated posture but with differing pairs of attendants to either side of the Buddha. The attendants include: Brahma and Indra, a variety of paired devas, demons, kinnaras, and rishis (hermits). The text is in Pali and contains the usual seven extracted texts from the Abhidhamma scriptures. An eighth painting depicts Phra Malai in heaven with the god Indra, and another shows a group of laymen seated in a pavilion.

The text on the reverse side of the manuscript, in Thai, is of the Phra Malai story. A colophon at the end of the text says that the book was made in B.E. 2423, equal to AD 1880. This type of Thai Buddhist manuscript illustration with a series of seated Buddha images became popular in the nineteenth century.

Raman microscopy analysis of this manuscript has identified many of the pigments used, including red lead, vermilion, chalk, white lead, ultramarine blue and carbon. These are not chemical dyes, although Thai artists had access to chemically synthesized dyes by 1880, when this manuscript was made.

PHRA MALAI

The legend of Phra Malai became the most popular subject of illustrated Buddhist manuscripts in nineteenth century Thailand. Neighbouring Buddhist countries such as Cambodia and Burma did not produce illustrated manuscripts of this Buddhist legend. Its earlier history in Thailand in the seventeenth and eighteenth centuries is obscure. A few examples can be attributed to the eighteenth century on the basis of style. It is possible that the Phra Malai legend itself only became popular in the Bangkok period, and then many illustrated manuscripts were made of it.

The story of Phra Malai, the monk who travels to heaven and hell by the powers he achieved through meditations and great merit, may find its origins in Srilanka, but it was composed in southeast Asia and is best known in Thailand. Seven subjects, shown in pairs, are nearly always included in the Thai illustrated Phra Malai manuscripts: (1) devas (or gods) at the beginning of the text, (2) monks attended by laymen, (3) hell scenes showing punishments, (4) a lotus picking scene, (5) the stupa in heaven containing the Buddha's relics, where Phra Malai offers the lotus picked by the poor woodcutter and engages in discussion with the god Indra, (6) heavenly beings (devas) floating in the air, and (7) a scene of evil people fighting contrasted with one of good people meditating in caves.

Many illustrated manuscripts of the Phra Malai story were made in central Thailand, particularly in the nineteenth century. It was widely used as a preaching text for funerals and weddings. The descriptions of heaven and hell vividly reminded the assembled community of the future awaiting them in heaven or hell, and of the punishments resulting from sinful behaviour. The story culminates in heaven with the appearance of Sri Ariya Maitreya, the Buddha of the future (in Thai, *Phra Si An*).

The Phra Malai text was recited by monks who would often embellish and dramatize their tellings, contrary to the rules for good behaviour of a monk. These highly popular, if undignified, performances were periodically forbidden by decrees banning monks from reciting the Phra Malai story. As a result former monks often delivered the recitations, dressed up as monks for the occasion, unconstrained by the rules of proper behaviour for monks.

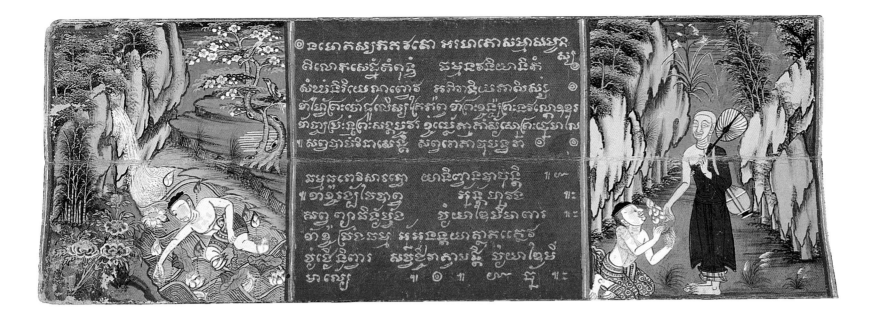

50 Phra Malai.

Chester Beatty Library (Dublin), Thai MS. 1328.

Folding book manuscript of khoi paper, with ten paired illustrations. 64 × 11.2 cm. 84 ff. Lacquered and gilt covers, with dragons and foliage.

Thai text (Phra Malai), in thin Cambodian script in gold and black ink.

Apparently dating from the end of the eighteenth century, this may be one of the earliest-known illustrated Phra Malai manuscripts. Based on the sombre background colours, the figure types that are close to those in the dated examples of 1776 and 1780, and the intermediate dimensions which fall between the narrower Ayutthaya manuscript size and the larger format of the nineteenth century (see p. 14 and note on p. 72), we can probably attribute this work to the late eighteenth century. The use of the thin form of Cambodian script is also consistent with such a date. The script is mainly written in gold letters on a rich red ground, a luxurious feature. Sumptuous lacquered and gilt covers, with superb dragons, monster faces, and scrolling foliage, adorn the outside of the manuscript. Within, a mastery of brilliant colouring combined with surreal rock formations conjure up a natural world of fantasy of compelling beauty.

The normal Phra Malai subjects are illustrated: (1). the monk Phra Malai receiving alms from country folk, (2). Phra Malai accepting a lotus bouquet from the woodcutter which he will carry up to heaven, and (3). the monk in heaven conversing with the god Indra, with (4). other angels and divinities in heaven. (5). In the underworld Phra Malai observes the condemned spirits.

In the first page of the manuscript the woodcutter picks lotus flowers to present to Phra Malai to carry to heaven above. At a later date, Phra Malai manuscripts almost always begin with the convention of paired deva figures on decorated thrones [see p. 98]. They

accompany the Pali language Buddhist scriptural extracts that normally precede the Phra Malai text. Here only the first three lines of text are in Pali and then the Thai text commences.

On the left (above), the lotus lake is richly embellished with a waterfall, mountains and forests. Planes are juxtaposed in the complex composition without any use of perspective. The prominent peony plant and the flowering tree with birds are both conventions deriving from Chinese painting and typical of the eighteenth-century Thai style. The right-hand scene, where the bouquet is presented to Phra Malai, is a stark one, with sheer cliffs and a deep blue sky behind. Phra Malai's eyes have not been painted in, for some reason.[1]

The next two scenes (pp. 94–5) complement the first two. To the left, two kinnaras (half-bird, half-humans) disport themselves in the Himavanta region in a clearing before cliffs and woods. Two fruit shaped objects lie on raised ground behind them. Their postures and adornments are particularly delicate. On the right side of the page Phra Malai flies through the air bearing the lotus bouquet, surrounded by a huge aureole which is finely decorated.

The last scenes in this book (pp. 96–7) depict, on the left, villagers presenting alms to the monk. Their house is set in an enchanted complex of rockery and forest. Phra Malai appears again in flight in the upper right corner. The elaborate structure of the painting and the rich colouring are highly effective. To the right, Phra Malai is seated in heaven conversing with the gods, within a double enclosure with green and blue gates. Two rows of heavenly beings fan out below the three main figures in an inventive, bold pattern.

[1] A possible link may be seen in a passage of mural painting of the late eighteenth century at Wat Chomphuwek where cliffs rise up dramatically. See N. Na Paknam 1987.

Phra Malai flying to heaven. Chester Beatty Library, Thai MS. 1328.

សត្យេញ៉យទ្បី វិកាបរ:
ត្យសនៈទ្បីលេបើទៅា
ព្រពញ៉ខព្រះអារទា
រ្យ៉ុុព្រះហារទាតាត់ូ២ខែ
ក្ខូុ២្បេវ្រឆេ ្សេរា:
រ្យ្ខៃវសទ្បាយ៉ូ្បេ២្ម៉ិ:

ារោៃគ្ឈសរ ត្ក្រ្ត:
ួិ្ទ្បុុៃ្រសុច្ច៉ឆៃ ២ហា:
ឆ្ួុ៉ៃៅ វេប្ថ្យៃវុ ភុ្សល
ប្ត្រ្សល្រៅ្ព្រះ់ា់ៃ
ត្ូៃៃវ៉ខ្ច្ព្រាួ្ហ្ញ
ួ្ុតតាបុ្តុ្ព្រ:ឯុ ្ពាួ

Villagers offering alms, and Phra Malai in heaven. Chester Beatty Library, Thai MS. 1328.

ភ្លើនៃព្រៃ ត្រិ៍ឧត្តា ទុបត្រាំ
នៃឃ្លិឍសូធ ។ ហា
សឞ្ច រឞ្សព្រះធម្ម ព្រះកោ៖
កាំខ្មែរឃេត្តកព្រះចោបឍ្ឍុល
មា ចុសុតឍស្សរគា អាឍិស្
កាឍិស្កុម្ភ្រៃប្ឈើអឍ ឲ្ឈេយ

ក្យរ្ក្ម្ម ឞឍក្ភុឍ្ធព៖
គាគាឍិញ្ញព្រះអាលៃធាំស្ព
៖មាលៃឞ្យ៍សេឞ្ចុបរិមុណ្ណ៖
ៗ មាលៃៈថាអ្ភរហឍោគា
ឍាឍ្មរាឍ៍ ។ ឈ្មេរៃៃហាឈ្យេ
ឌ្ៃ ឍ្ញាកព្រះឍេឞ្សរគា ៕៖

51 Phra Malai.

New York Public Library, Thai MS. 22.

Folding book manuscript of khoi paper, with 24 paired illustrations. 67 cm wide.

Although providing no information on when it was made, this striking manuscript has the main characteristics of early nineteenth century Thai painting – dark background colours, large scale of figures, and distinctive draughtsmanship with firm yet still relatively fluid lines. At the same time the painting here has an unrefined provincial quality similar in some ways to 52 and 53, and distinct from the 'court style' of 41.

The manuscript opens with paired figures on plinths or thrones, a standard feature of the nineteenth century Phra Malai books. Above are lesser divinities, and below, hermits. Here they boldly fill the frame of the picture on blue and green grounds, whereas later in the century they will be smaller in scale. The pairs of figures may be limited to one or two pairs, or may also spread over many succeeding openings of the manuscript.

The scenes in heaven are also standard ones, but rendered here on dramatic black grounds richly set with golden blossoms (p. 100): Phra Malai and other heavenly beings floating in the air (on right) and Phra Malai in heaven at the Chulamani stupa adorned with hamsa standards and lizard banners(above, left) and conversing with the god Indra (below, left). A final detail (p. 101) is a distinctively provincial variant of the lotus picking scene, with the pond enclosed in a red outlined frame and behind it an oddly stylized tree against a brown ground. Beside it lies the woodcutter's knife.

ន្ធុំទាំងអ្វីនៃមហាសមុទ្រ

កងការ កម្ពុះសហារ

ព្រះស្មុទ្រសាគរ ១

យុគ្គរ ៈយុឌ័នៃគេរ ◉

មុតឆ្លុងសីវ្យ ◉ ឧព្រះហេ

ទ្វេឆ្លើទ្វេស្លើ គេនក្ញ

ស្វានុំ ◉ ន័ំនៃសាគ៌រអ្យ្រ្ត្ន

ជ្រីឈៈហេុបើ្រិតហវ្យ ◉

ព្រះសឹ្រនៅ្យបម្ង្ហ្ឆៀយ ១ ព្រះហេ

នាឌ័ក្ញ្យ ្រ្គ្រ៌ិយ្ស្ងុហ្វ ◉

ឫ មឹបរិឃារ យេ្ងុស្ងឺ

ឫ បំ្រ្ក្ភ្កេ្ភៅ ៈមន្ងៈ ◉

ំេ្ ្រ្ភ្ណំ េ្ឆេៈ្ពារ

េ្ភ្រ្ឬ្ហ្ ្ឧ្ភ្ឆ្ញ៌ ◉

ឫ្ ្រ្ ្គ្រ្ ្រ្ ្រ្ ្រ្ ្រ្ ្រ្ ្រ្ ្រ្ ្ ◉

◉ ្ ្គ្នេសរ្រ្េ ្ ្ ្្្្្្្្ ្្្

្្្្្្្្ ្្ ◉ ្្្ ្្

្្្្្ ្្ ្្្្ ្្

្្្្្ ្្្្ ្្្

្្្ ្្្ ្្្្ ◉

Phra Malai in heaven. New York Public
Library, Thai MS. 22.

Woodcutter picks lotuses to give to Phra Malai.
New York Public Library, Thai MS. 22.

52 Phra Malai, dated 1837.

British Library, Oriental and India Office Collections. Or. 14710.

Folding book manuscript of khoi paper with with six paired illustrations, 37 cm. wide. Brown lacquered covers. Thai text (Phra Malai) written in thin Cambodian script.

An expressive elongation of figures and limbs marks this artist's work. The manuscript has a colophon dated to 1199 in the Chula era, equivalent to 1837.

There are only six paintings in all, fewer than usual for a Phra Malai manuscript. They illustrate hell, heaven, and the lotus-picking scene. The backgrounds are quite dark, or occasionally pale.

The scene of the woodcutter in the pond is densely worked, with rocks and trees behind the woodcutter in the pond, against a rising bank. The artist does not attempt to indicate receding space, except with the bank which rises vertically behind the cutout edge of the shore. Water is indicated by the traditional curved lines. The woodcutter in the pond is highly stylized, with puppet-like limbs, while Phra Malai looms up on the right. In fact there are no specifically 'modern' elements in this style at all. The artist, a superb craftsman of line and colours, was either unfamiliar with, or uninterested in, new trends of the 1830s.

The text is unusual for omitting the usual Pali scripture extracts at the beginning of the manuscript, and containing only the Phra Malai text. The script is more cursive in style than usual in this type of manuscript.

53 Phra Malai, dated 1839.

New York Public Library, Spencer Collection. Thai MS. 12.

Folding book manuscript of khoi paper, with ten paired illustrations, 67.5 cm. wide. Cambodian script in black ink.

Another Phra Malai manuscript, dated only two years after the last example, also seems to continue earlier styles, with backgrounds that are solid bright colours – yellow, red, and blue. Such deep coloured backgrounds were particularly employed from the late eighteenth century onward. The landscape scenes in this example on the other hand have dark grounds in the newer style. Flowers decorate the solid grounds. In figures, the lines are rather stiff, with attenuated shapes as seen in the previous manuscript, but rendered with somewhat less sophistication. The effect of these figures is affecting, however, in a similar way. The gold and lacquer covers of the manuscript are filled with scrolling foliage, flowers, and large birds.

On the first illustrations two elegant devas are seated on either side of the page, rendered with detail that is relatively simple, but the colouring is sensitive and highly effective, as so often in Thai painting.

The artist presents the usual Phra Malai scenes in a conventional way, but also includes the subject of a funeral. A funeral scene is of course appropriate since Phra Malai texts were recited mainly at funerals. On the right a funeral pyre blazes, while a monk attends to the corpse in the coffin on the left, with grieving mourners on both sides. As with the 1837 example there are no particularly 'modern' elements in this style.

We can conclude from these two dated Phra Malai manuscripts, and others, that different Thai artists at any one particular period worked in a variety of styles and varying degrees of modernization.

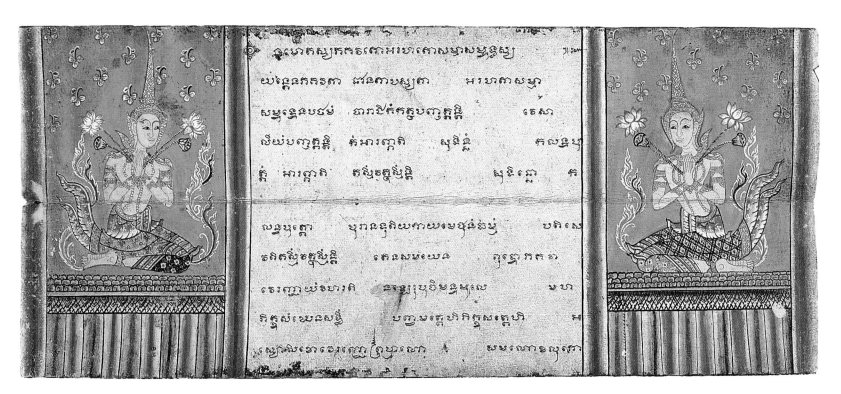

ទុមហាកស្សកគគេាអរហាកាលម្មាសម្ពុទ្ធស្ស

យបន្ទេនកគនា ឯនគាបស្សេត   អរហាគលម្ម
សម្ពុន្ធនបឋម   ឆាជេកែកភ្ងបញ្ញត្តិ   ទេសេ
លិយបញ្ញត្តិ   កំអារញ្ញាគ   សុនិន្ត្ត   កលន្ធុ
ក្ត   អារញ្ញាគ   គស្មិទក្ខុស្ំន្ និ   សុនិ ជ្ឈោ   គ

លន្ធុក្ត្គា   បុរនឆុគិយកាយមេធុន្ធិអ្ំ   បគសេ
រគិគស្មិទក្ខុស្ំ និ   គេនសមយេន   ភុន្ត្ថេាកគន
ទេរញ្ញាយ៍ឧហារគ   នឧ្ទ្ធ្រុបុឆិមឧ្នុស្សេ   មហា
កគុស្ំ ឈេនឧស្ន្និ   បញ្ញមគ្លេាជីកិភ្ងុសភ្លុហិ   អ
ស្មាលិសឹនាទេនេរេញ្ញ ព្រះ្ឆណា   ។   សមណោឧុ្ភ្គា

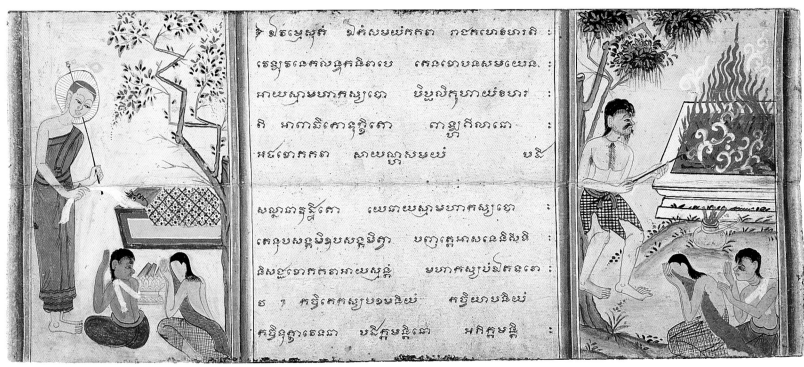

ន ឧិនម្ដ្មេសុគ   ៗគំសមយ៍កគនា   រាគគហេឧហារគ ៈ
ទេឧ្យ៍ទនេគសន្ទគិនាបេ   គេនឌោរូឧនសមយេន ៈ
អាយស្មាមហាកស្សបោ   បិឌ្ឌសិភ្ងុហាយ៍ឧហារ
គ   អាគានិកោឧទ្ធិតោ   ៗឈ្លាបិណោ   ៈ
អឌ្លោកគនា   សាយស្មាសមយ៍   ឧ ៈ

សន្ទានគ្ពុ្ដ្ដិគោ   យេនាយស្មាមហាកស្សបោ ៈ
គេឧបសន្ទិឌុបសន្ទមិ្គ្ំ   បញ្ញគ្លេអាសនេនិសិឌិ ៈ
និឧ្ទ្ធោគគនាអាយសុឌ្ំ   មមហាកស្សប៉ឌគនទេា
ា   ។។   គឌ្ញិគេគស្សបឧ្ឧមនិយ៍   គឌ្ញិយាឧនិយ៍
គឌ្ញិឧ្ទ្ធានេននា   បឌិ្គ្ភ្ងមន្ធិ្នោ   អគគ្គមន្ធិ្ ៈ

Seated devas (*above*) and funeral scenes (*below*).
New York Public Library, Thai MS. 12.

Woodcutter picks lotuses to give to Phrai Malai.
British Library, Or. 14838. Dated to 1849.

ឱ្យសេចក្ដីបវ នៃ្យុវនិការហ្ន
ឧយសុវរ ទៃុលេក្ឆ្លាតៃ
ក្នុងស្ម្មាម លើ្យខ្លព្រមាញ្ញ
ឡ្យខព្រមាញ្ញ តាយាឧរ៕
ឡ្រ្លាឧបញ្ច ៃេឫ្ឈ្លោសៃភា
ថ

ញ្ញតាមព្រាជ្ឈហា ឫ្ឫ្ពៃៃេ្រ
អុហាេតេក្ឆ្ល សំុមត្ថ្រៃយ
ត
ឡ្វិញិធី ឫុឡសាេនាៃសៃ
ៈថៃេនាបវ ឡ្យៃេ្តកុសញ្ច
ក្ខុសញ្ច េតេព្រមាៃេ

សាធម្ម៍ពិសាសាប្

នុនព័ងរញ្ញក្រ:ស្យ
ស្រួងសនោះព្រោះឲ្យចេ
ម្ងៃននសម្បុរ្ព្រះសិរអរិយ

ទេ្ខមាចេនេនសម្មុណា
មាប្ដីម្ងៃននុនេសម្ងៃនព្ណ
ព្រមាច:ឥអន្តៃនៃម្ងៃនសុរ
ប្រ:មានសទេ្ឌពបិត្ត
ទុករប៉ូព័្យទ្បាច្ច្រ រាមាចេ

ទុករនាធ្មហាយ
ចព្ង័តក្ស្ញព្រ:សិរអរិយ
ចព្ង័តព៍ធម្មុនេតមហា
ចព្ងៃព្រ:និព្ផាន
ចទេ្ឌទ្ធុបេក្ផា

ខ្ម្ងៃ្ព្យ្កុសន្ម្ម
ចព្ប្រែតបិត្ត
ចទេ្ឌ្យនរបុញ្ញ

✤ ៕ ព្រ:មាសេយ្យួ្រ
ឡ្យមាឥ៌សេនេន្ម្ពិន្ទ្ប៊ម្រាច៍ព៌ិ

54 Phra Malai, dated 1849.

Folding book manuscript of khoi paper with sixteen paired illustrations. 66 cm. wide.

British Library, Oriental and India Office Collections. Or. 14838.

Pali text (extracts from Abhidhamma scriptures) and Thai text (Phra Malai) written in thin Cambodian script. Colophon (dated to 1849) at end of text, written in Thai script.

The virtuoso painting in this manuscript is the work of a very fine artist, but he is not mentioned in the dated colophon which lists the names of the donors. They are a mother and her two children, and it is stated that they paid for the making of the manuscript as well as for fabric to wrap it in, and a lacquered and gilt chest in which to keep it. The total cost was eight tamlung two baht one fuang.

The 'super real' style, with natural details rendered with the sharpest accuracy, reflects influence from abroad, perhaps Indian or European. This type of realistic representation was not a traditional element of Thai painting. Each scene is rendered in exquisite detail.

The composition of the lotus picking scene (pp. 104–105) is traditional in its elements. The artist has not attempted to depict space behind the immediate scene, as artists will soon be doing in the 1850s and 1860s in the style of western landscapes. But the rendering of surface details and the colouring are quite exceptional in their realism.

The satirical scene of false monks, reciting the Phra Malai text when ordained monks were forbidden from doing so, and with laymen seated below them (including two playing a board game) is also a familiar one, but the delicate characterization of the figures, the colouring, shading, and quality of detail, are all exceptional in Thai painting of this period. The high level of sophistication is surprising at a time when most artists were adhering to traditional norms.

The date given, 2392 in the Buddhist era, the year of the Monkey, is equivalent to 1849 AD, at the end of the reign of King Rama III.

55 Phra Malai (and the Ten Birth Tales).

British Library, Oriental and India Office Collections, Or. 14559.

Folding book manuscript of khoi paper with 32 paired illustrations, 67.5 cm wide.

Pali text (extracts from Abhidhamma scriptures) and Thai text (Phra Malai) written in thin Cambodian script. Colophon (undated) in Thai script.

Although unsophisticated and somewhat rustic in style, a rich visual imagination has produced some startling, unexpected images in this manuscript. The artist has set rectangular frames around each scene, perhaps under western influence, as if within a picture frame. Phra Malai hovers above the denizens of hell. They are truly fearful creatures, with foetus-like bony bodies and huge skulls with big eyes. A demure buffalo-headed ghoul sits on the left. The lotus pond is also a rather threatening place here. Huge lotus leaves dwarf the woodcutter as he collects a bouquet, and two raucous birds peck at his head.

Dating perhaps from the 1860s or 1870s, this manuscript also includes illustrations of the Ten Birth Tales. At the end of the text a colophon, without a date, identifies the sponsors of the book, Pho Phlai and his wife Mae Thap. They make typical requests that they and their parents may benefit from the merit of sponsoring the book, escaping from the world and its cycle of rebirths, and that they might reach heaven where they would meet Maitreya, the Buddha of the Future, and see the stupa holding the Buddha's relics.

រស្សូបិយុម្ព្រោ
ទុងិស្សូនស្បាន ៖
កប្ប្រន១មាន
ព្រោះញាប្តិ១កាំ ៖
ខ្ទិស្សាតម្ល ហោម្ប្រីធម្ម
ព្រប្ចូនបារ៍ប ៖
ព្រះធេរមាន៍ស្សូ
ម្ចិខ្ពូប្រ ៖
របេតា ហោប្ល្តិម្ព្រាណ៍
ម្ប្រៀ ៖ ◎ ន្ប្រ ◎

ប្រីស្ទេច្ចៅ៍ប ឡរិក្ស្បារ ៖
ម្ចិខ្ពយស្សូរ ទុស្ងេ្ញ្តាខ្ទ្ម ៖
ក្ស្លជ្ញ្ម្តម្ល ស្ប្ៀជ្ព្រះមារតា ៖
មស្ប្ៀជ្ព្រះមាតាញ្ចយ្ជ្ជានវពល្ច ៖
ហេ្ចូកខុច្ច ម្ប្ច្ត្វូក្ន៍សេ៣ ៖
មមាខ្ពយ៍ច ស១្រាជ្ចូ្ផ្វៃ៍យ្សូរ
មស្ប្ៀ៍ក្ន្ម្រាពេខ្ត្ក្ន្ស្រ្រ្ម្នព្ចេ៍ស្ស
ម្វិ្ងម្ចៅ្ផ្ព្វ្ចិ្ត្ម ម្ចិ្នស្បាខ្ចូ៍ស្សូ ៖
ព្រះធេរមាន៍ស្ស្បូ ៖
ខ្ពយ៍ច្បក៍ន៍ស្សណ៍

56 Phra Malai, dated 1897.

Chester Beatty Library (Dublin), Thai MS. 1319.

Folding book manuscript of khoi paper with 22 paired illustrations, 67 cm wide. Black lacquer covers with gold leaf decoration.

Thai text (the Phra Malai legend), in thin Cambodian script in black ink.

Even at the very end of the Thai manuscript tradition fine artists produced work of great artistic merit. Although quite standard in type this manuscript is carefully and finely painted. It is dated to 1897, the year when King Chulalongkorn made his first tour of European nations. By this date many reforms had been effected, and western cultural influence was considerable.

We see (above) Phra Malai in heaven, seated on a terrace with divinities. It is treated in perspective, and shadows are cast by the heavenly standards and a gas lamp-post onto the background wall. The landscape scenes below depict, on the left, the contrast between meditation and strife during the age of evil, which is usually shown in two scenes but here was combined into one. On the right is a scene from the 'golden age' with gems falling off trees, before a landscape that is fully westernized in type.

57 Phra Malai, dated 1903.

British Library Or. 15370 and another example (Private Collection, Bangkok)

Folding book manuscripts of khoi paper, each 68 × 15 cm. Each with 22 paired illustrations.

By the latter part of the nineteenth century a practice of nearly exact copying of Phra Malai manuscripts was introduced. The evidence for this is found in a number of nearly identically illustrated manuscripts. The two examples compared here provide clear evidence of this practice. The lower of the two manuscripts is dated to 1903 AD, close to the end of the Thai manuscript tradition.

It is apparent that the basic details are the same in the two manuscripts. The text was also copied quite exactly, largely in the same positions on the page. The individual artist was still free to fill in the details, but the basic format of the pictures was apparently fixed. We do not know if they were made several at a time on a studio basis, or one at a time. It would seem that the dated example of 1903 is the later of the two examples, based on the somewhat drier, harder character of the painting. Yet even with the confines of the prescribed model, the details and colours are beautifully realized in both manuscripts.

On the pages shown the denizens of heaven are floating in the air, on the left four hermits, and on the right as crowd of angels below the single figure of the great Maitreya, the Buddha of the future, surrounded by an aureole. The Thai text on this page describes the arrival of Maitreya with his retinue and the offerings made at the heavenly sites.

COSMOLOGY

Traditional Thai Buddhist concepts explained the nature and appearance of the universe. These concepts were drawn from texts in the Pali language, and were compiled in a Thai language version called Traiphum [literally 'three worlds']. Surviving copies of the full text date only from the late eighteenth century but represent a text that dates back to several centuries earlier.

Traiphum manuscripts were often lavishly illustrated, with diagrams of the world, the heavens and hells, and also with Buddhist narratives, mainly of the life of the Buddha and of the previous lives of the Buddha. Two Traiphum manuscripts, both dated to to the year 1776 AD, are among the best survivals of old Thai manuscript painting. One of them was brought to Berlin by the scholar Adolf Bastian and given to the Museum für Volkerkunde there in 1893, while the other is preserved in the National Library, Bangkok. (See Wenk 1965 and *Buddhist Cosmology* 1982).

58 Thai Buddhist Cosmology (Traiphum), dated 1805.

Chester Beatty Library, Dublin. Thai MS. 1355.
Folding book manuscript of khoi paper, 75 folds.
37 cm wide. Text in Thai script in black ink.

This illustrated Traiphum manuscript from the
Chester Beatty Library in Dublin is dated to 1805.
It contrasts strongly with the 1776 examples (see
note on p. 72) in its sketchy painting style,
probably provincial workmanship, and in the less
extensive treatment of the subject. A possible
explanation for the difference in style between this
example and the far more elegant 1776 manuscripts
is that the date of 1805 may be copied from an
earlier manuscript, rather than recording the year in
which it was itself made.

 The illustration here of the Tavatimsa heaven is
identified by a caption at the top reading: 'this
is Tavatimsa at the top of Mt Sumeru, the residence
of Lord Indra.' Indra's pavilion is supported by the
three-headed elephant vehicle of Indra named
Erawan, and next to it is the Chulamani pagoda that
enshrines the sacred relic of the Buddha.

The Buddha's footprints,
from a cosmology manuscript
dated 1903.
New York Public Library.
Thai MS. 25.

พระบาทอยู่กลาง
พระมหาสมุทพระมาก
บซนเลพน
ป

59

59 Thai Buddhist Cosmology (Traiphum), dated 1903.

New York Public Library, Thai MS. 25.

Folding book manuscript of khoi paper, 37.5 cm wide. Text in Thai; Thai script in black ink.

If the date 1903 that appears in this manuscript, which is suprisingly written in roman numerals in the Christian era, is in fact the year in which it was made, then for its date is quite traditional in type and has relatively little that is 'modern' or westernized in its style.

One scene depicts footprints of the Buddha, important objects of veneration in the Buddhist faith, where the Buddha is believed to have walked during his life. The site of one footprint is a major pilgrimage place, in Saraburi province north of Bangkok. The manuscript depicts two such footprints, one (above) which is identified by the text as the 'desert' footprint. Next to it a travelling monk is seated with his alms bowl, parasol, and shoulder bag for travel. The text says: 'a monk eating a meal at the bank of the Yamuna river'. In the forests to the right, monkeys tease a tiger from a tree above and, at the far right, a tiger attacks a cow. The second footprint is identified by the text above on the right as 'the footprint in the great sea'. A variety of curious sea and land creatures swim toward the footprint to pay homage to it. A mermaid and merman couple hold lotuses above the footprint to honour it. The water is rendered in the traditional way with patterns of curved lines.

A second painting indicates the four great continents of men that are situated within the great oceans, at the cardinal directions from the foot of the central cosmic mountain (Mount Meru). For each continent a male and female couple represent the inhabitants, with a tree that is emblematic of that continent. The text identifies details about each continent, such as its distance from the central mountain, the lifespan of its people, etc. Below, we find the northern continent which is said to be 80,000 yojanas from the centre. Its inhabitants live for a thousand years, and the native tree is the *kamaphruk* tree. To the right is the western continent, only 7000 yojanas distant, where the people live for 100 years.

60 Thai Buddhist Cosmology (Traiphum).

British Library, Oriental and India Office Collections. Or. 15245.

Folding book manuscript of khoi paper, 37 × 13.5 cm. Text in Pali [entitled Dhammasangini] in Cambodian script in black ink, and in Thai [Traiphum] in Thai script in purple ink. *c.*1900–1920.

After the mid nineteenth century the prestige of the old Thai cosmology text was seriously challenged by western ideas and by the introduction of modern geography. Yet traditional cosmology manuscripts were still produced, and this very late example seems to date from early in the twentieth century. Raman spectrometry examination has identified a number of chemically synthesized dye colours, such as chrome white, chrome yellow, and acquamarine, different from the natural dye colours of traditional manuscripts.[1]

The heavens are depicted as pavilions with identifying captions in Cambodian script. An inscription in Thai in the mountain section of the painting gives the name of the scribe as Nai Sun.

[1] Burgio 1999.

60

61 Phra Tham [Protective Formulas].

John Rylands University Library of Manchester Thai Ms. 1.

Folding book manuscript of khoi paper, 44 × 11 cm. 47 folds.

Text in Cambodian script in gold (Pali language) and yellow (Thai language) ink. Lavishly decorated on side one in gold and rich colours on a blue ground; on side two, text only on a black ground. Wooden covers, incised and silvered, with foliage, birds and two kinnaras. Mid-nineteenth century.

The elegant quality and format of this book containing Buddhist protective formulas is unusual, and no other finely-executed example has been encountered of this subject. Although entitled Phra Tham, literally *dhamma* or the teachings of the Buddha, the manuscript contains not texts from the Buddhist canon, but diagrams composed from syllables of text. These constitute yantras, magical diagrams which were used by knowledgeable monks or men who practised occult arts, for protection or to help achieve specific goals.

The syllables and letters of the Cambodian alphabet were mysterious to all but the most learned students of Buddhism, and were imbued with the sacred power of the religion, and therefore effective towards the attainment of a desired goal. The construction of such formulas from syllables of sacred Pali texts is explained in detail in a Cambodian study (Bizot and Hinuber 1994).

This lavish manuscript was made for a wealthy patron. In the large opening diagram a small seated Buddha without facial features is surrounded by gold letters, then coloured bands in red, white, and gold, carefully inscribed with magic formulas. Below the Buddha image are two attendants to the far left and right, and directly below, two golden diagrams and head drawn from the art of the Ramakian dance-drama in the form of a stylized monkey.

Another diagram is in the form of a sectioned sphere intersected by red pillars with multiple gold finials. Below it an elegant lion stands in a red panel set within green, gold and blue rectangles.

FORTUNE-TELLING

Fortune-tellers were widely consulted by the whole of society in old Thailand. Illustrated fortune-telling books were commissioned from painters to aid in the prognostication. The system of fortune-telling was based simply on the day and month of birth of the user. The illustrations in the manuscripts depict a rich variety of figures that are 'character types' or 'mascots', such as princes, animals, demons, or groups of paired figures. The text details the prospects for the client that are indicated by each mascot or mascot group.[1]

Illustrated fortune telling manuscripts were made in Thailand until the end of the nineteenth century, when they were replaced by printed texts. Relatively few illustrated manuscripts survive in good condition due to heavy use over many years, but examples in western collections tend to be better preserved, as they were often relatively new when brought from Thailand.

[1] For a detailed account of the contents of the texts, and methods used in Thai fortune-telling see Quaritch Wales 1983 who stated that nearly one thousand manuscripts on fortune-telling and astrology are kept in the National Library in Bangkok.

62 Fortune-Telling Manual.

British Library, Oriental and India Office Collections, Or. 14532.

Folding book manuscript of khoi paper, 42 × 16.5 cm. 30 folds. Late eighteenth or early nineteenth century. Mon script in black ink.

The contribution of the Mon peoples to the arts of Thailand throughout history has been a great one, but it has not always been clearly defined, particularly in recent centuries. This Mon fortune-telling book is illustrated in the same format as a Thai one, and its painting is very similar to the style of late eighteenth century Thailand, characterized by its figures, great vitality in the drawing, and simple, vivid colouring. But this manuscript comes from Burma rather than Thailand, and was brought to Scotland at the time of the Anglo-Burmese wars in the 1820s. A distinctive group of Burmese and Thai manuscripts of the late eighteenth and early nineteenth centuries in the British Library are related closely in style to this Mon manuscript, and reflect the interaction of the two regions following the destruction of Ayutthaya in 1767. Artists were brought as captives from Thailand to Burma, and some or most of these artists may have been Mon. This manuscript is likely to be direct evidence of the work and influence of these transported artists.[1] An inscription in English on the first page states: 'This manuscript was procured at Rangoon by Mr Stewart the Medical officer attached to Mr Crawfurd's Mission – It is said to be written in the old Taleen (or Pegu) language for which Mr Stewart could obtain no explanation. 14 March 1827.'

The years of the tiger and the hare are represented as usually, with four variant tigers and hares, and as a presiding mascot figure seated on a pedestal by the tree associated with that year. A variant form of fortune-telling employs figures of a horse, elephant, and intertwined serpents to lead to the correct fortune.

[1] Another manuscript very similar in format and illustrations that clearly belongs to the work of the artists transplanted to Burma, but written in Burmese and Thai rather than Mon, is also in the British Library, Or. 12167.

The years of the tiger and
the hare.
(British Library, Or. 14532.)

စံပယ်ကၠိပတဲ့ ရွိုင်ပိုးမ္ဥ္းဥ ဂၤဗု

အသက်ြ ပ တဲ့ မတၠ်ကၠ္ဍာက်
သဝရိုကၠ်ပဖ္ဲ ဖွိကၠ်ကၠ်ကၠကၠ်
ဘတ ဖိကၠုပုဲ့

အသုတၠ်ၐ ပတဲ့ ကိုန္ဍ လ ၐ
ဂ ထကၠ်ကၠ်
ဖြ္ဍ သ္ဥ ၐ ၐ ၐ ၐ တု ဥ ၐ

ပုၣ်မ်ပတၠ်ရ ဂိုန္ဍ ဝတ
ရို ဖြဖ္ဍိ ခၠ်ၐ တု သုက္ခာတ္
ရ္ဥ

ၐ ရ
ၐ ၐ ၐ ၐ ၐ ၐ ၐ ၐ ၐ ၐ ၐ ၐ ၐ ၐ ၐ ၐ ၐ ၐ ၐ
ၐ ၐ ၐ ၐ ၐ ၐ ၐ ၐ ၐ ၐ ၐ ၐ ၐ ၐ ၐ ၐ ၐ ၐ ၐ
ၐ ၐ ၐ ၐ ၐ ၐ ၐ ၐ ၐ ၐ ၐ ၐ ၐ ၐ ၐ ၐ ၐ ၐ ၐ
ၐ ၐ ၐ ၐ ၐ ၐ ၐ ၐ ၐ ၐ ၐ ၐ ၐ ၐ ၐ ၐ ၐ ၐ
ၐ ၐ ၐ ၐ ၐ ၐ ၐ ၐ ၐ ၐ ၐ ၐ ၐ ၐ ၐ ၐ ၐ ၐ

63 Fortune-Telling Manual.

British Library, Oriental and India Office Collections, I.O. Siamese 18.

Folding book manuscript of khoi paper, 17.5 × 12.5 cm. 63 folds. Thai script in black ink.

The small, more square, format of this manuscript is a southern Thai type, called 'elephant-foot book' (*but tin chang*) in the southern dialect. The fortune-telling contents are also southern in type, consisting of a scene from Thai literature to accompany each fortune; in southern dialect it is called *saatraa*. A stick on a string was swung freely until it stopped at a particular page of the open book, thus choosing the fortune. Another way was to insert a knife randomly into the closed book to select a page. The many scenes in the illustrations, 63 in all, form a summary of literature that was popular in old Thailand. The language used in the text is also in the southern Thai dialect.

A scene from the Ramakian (right), the Thai version of the Indian epic the Ramayana, shows the monkey ruler Phraya Chumphu. The fortune on this page is a very good one: one will have the respect of others, as well as the mate of one's choice, and if things get lost they will soon be found.

A second fortune from the book (right) depicts the comic character Chuchok from the Vessantara tale lying on his bed suffering from the gross overindulgence in food and luxuries from which he will soon die. The fortune on this page predicts that a windfall is likely this year, and a wife can be sought, and if things are lost they should be looked for in the north.

A final example (far right) illustrates the story of Hoi Sang, the prince in a conch shell, where the executioner leads the character off to be killed.

Some of the paintings in this book are highly expressive although they are unsophisticated and somewhat uneven in quality. There is no background treatment and figures are set on the plain ground of the paper. The manuscript probably dates from the mid nineteenth century.

prospects, but there are no captions provided here to spell out the fortunes.

In a second illustration from this manuscript we find mascot groups for the years of the horse (left) and pig (right). The text identifies the month of birth so that the client can indentify the mascot group relevant to his or her fortune.

66 Fortune Telling Manual (c.1840).

Chester Beatty Library, MS. Thai 1302.

Folding book manuscript of khoi paper, 35 × 12 cm.

This elegant fortune-telling manuscript is accompanied by a translation into French dated 1847, by Bishop Pallegoix, the distinguished scholar and lexicographer of Thai. The translation

and the manuscript were presented by Pallegoix to a Portuguese gentleman, Senhor Marcellino D'Araujo Roza.

The year of the monkey and the year of the pig are shown here, each with four types of animal to identify the individual fortune depending on the month of birth of the user. To the right of the monkeys is the main mascot figure for the year of the monkey, in this case a green demon seated on a throne under a thorn tree. Similarly, to the right of the four pig types is the main mascot for the pig year, an elegant female on a throne under lotus leaves and flowers. The text summarizes various marital prospects for couples under these signs.

Six groups of figures on the left are relevant to the personal prospects
of those born in the year of the horse. Vessantara's wife and children
appear in the lower left. Six groups on the right are for the year of
the pig and include a fine elephant (*top right*) and a merman (in Thai,
ngu'ak, bottom right).

67 Fortune Telling Manual, dated 1885.

British Library, Oriental and India Office Collections, Or. 3593.
Folding book manuscript of khoi paper, 35 cm wide.

A Thai inscription at the beginning of this fortune-telling book states
that it was made for Mr French. E. H. French was the British consul in
Bangkok in the 1880s and 1890s, and the manuscript is dated to the
year 1885. Three years later in 1888 it was presented to the British
Museum by Sir Ernest Satow, the British Minister in Thailand. French
was described in a contemporary London newspaper c.1890 as 'a tall,
slim, and wily personage, the inspirer and confidant of Prince
Dewawongse, Minister of Foreign Affairs'. French corresponded with
George Curzon during the crucial years when it was feared that the
French might take over Siam. In one letter of 1893 he wrote to
Curzon: 'Mr Thompson, the Times Correspondent has been attacking
me with the greatest bitterness. He throws the whole blame of the
Siamese coming to terms with the French upon me as if the Siamese
would again after the Paknam affair defy the French single handed.'[1]

The groups of 'mascot' figures illustrate the prospects of marriage
partners, depending on their day and month of birth. For example the
mascot couple at the top left, a pair of local spirits, promise wealth
and great happiness throughout a very long life.

The careful and rather uninspired workmanship in this manuscript
is common in the later nineteenth century. A new palette of chemically
synthesized colours from Europe was by now readily available on the
market and replaced the traditional colour values of Thai painting.[2]

[1] British Library, Curzon Collection, Mss. Eur. F.111/81B, f.2, and F.111/87A
8.11.93

[2] Seven illustrations of this ms are reproduced in Wales, 1983, together with a
detailed account of the accompanying text.

๔๕ ฉนามประทุษภ้ย ลักขณะ ๔๐ งาแกงสีราคแม้น ยงคุน

ชื่อพัททพินายงา งอกนั้น งวกซ่นเอาขนายปุ่น เปรียบเท้

ยลเสมอสนับพลุกปก กฎแก่เกี่ยวแช เบื้องขวายสั้นเพชรพญ ทะระภาพ

ฉิแก่เบื้องซ้ายหั้น วิบัติภัยแมงผลาญ ชื่ออินทกินพินายแล้ สัปไว้ใหรุ่ทาย

68 Elephant Treatise.

Chester Beatty Library, Dublin. Thai MS. 1301.

Folding book manuscript of khoi paper, 39 × 13 cm., with wood covers inlaid in coloured glass. Dated 1816. 144 folds. Text in Thai script entirely in gold, on coloured grounds.

Thai treatises on elephants were produced by skilled court artists and kept by the official in charge of the crown's elephants. Loosely based on Indian elephant treatises, they describe a variety of elephants of both mythical and real types.

Elephants were of enormous importance in old Siam, in warfare as battle mounts, and in heavy work of many sorts. They were also an important export commodity and were regularly shipped to India for sale. Thai kings sought to capture and keep at court in luxurious splendour any 'white' elephants found in the wild (see p. 47). White elephants were regarded as talismans of the kingdom's prosperity.

A number of the surviving Thai elephant treatises bear dates in the second reign of the Bangkok era, such as one at the National Library Bangkok (1815), also the Chester Beatty Library (1816) and Berlin's Statsbibliothek (1819). They are all luxuriously produced.[1]

The Chester Beatty example is dated to the second day of the week, fifth of the waning moon of the first month in the year of the rat, 1178 in the Chula era, which is equivalent to 9 December 1816 AD. The colophon, written by the three scribes who give their names – Nai Duang, Nai Wen and Nai Niam, specifies that it was copied in gold script from an existing elephant manuscript in the palace that is framed in mother-of-pearl. The manuscript is accompanied by elaborate covers of wood, inlaid in coloured glass with floral designs between green and gold crosses. Nearly 150 elephants are illustrated and described in verse in the accompanying text.

Above, is the composite elephant made up of 26 devas, and related to the popular Indian composite paintings. Opposite is a page showing elephants from nature. They are called Hina and have many bad characteristics (*hina* means bad in Pali and Thai). One of them is eating shellfish at a pond here, and can be compared with a similar elephant in a somewhat later elephant treatise (Ginsburg: pl. 10).

[1] Two further examples, not dated, are reproduced in Ginsburg 1989: 33–43.

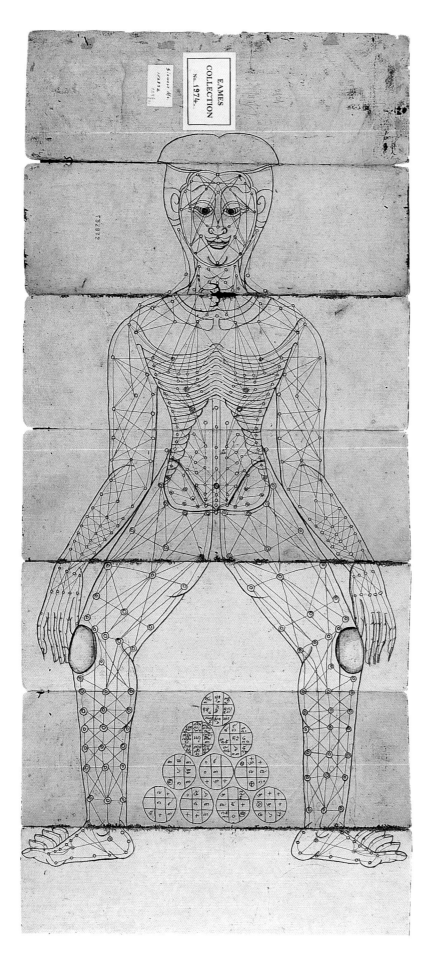

69 Pressure Massage Manual.

Wellcome Institute Library, London. Oriental Manuscripts: Siamese 801.

Folding book manuscript of khoi paper, 37.5 x 12.5 cm.

Finely-drawn human figures in this book indicate the location of pressure points for medical treatment. In the west, pressure massage is usually known by its Japanese name, 'shiatsu'. It probably reached Thailand from China where its use was also widespread. A school of medicine was established at Bangkok's Wat Pho in the 1830s, and this manuscript probably dates from that period.

The large unlabelled diagram indicates the essential lines in the body and the points on the surface at which treatment can be applied. In the second diagram information is given explaining what ailments can be treated at specific points. The figure is male and the point under his chin is for treating inability to eat or sleep. At the navel five ailments are treated including constipation and paralyses.

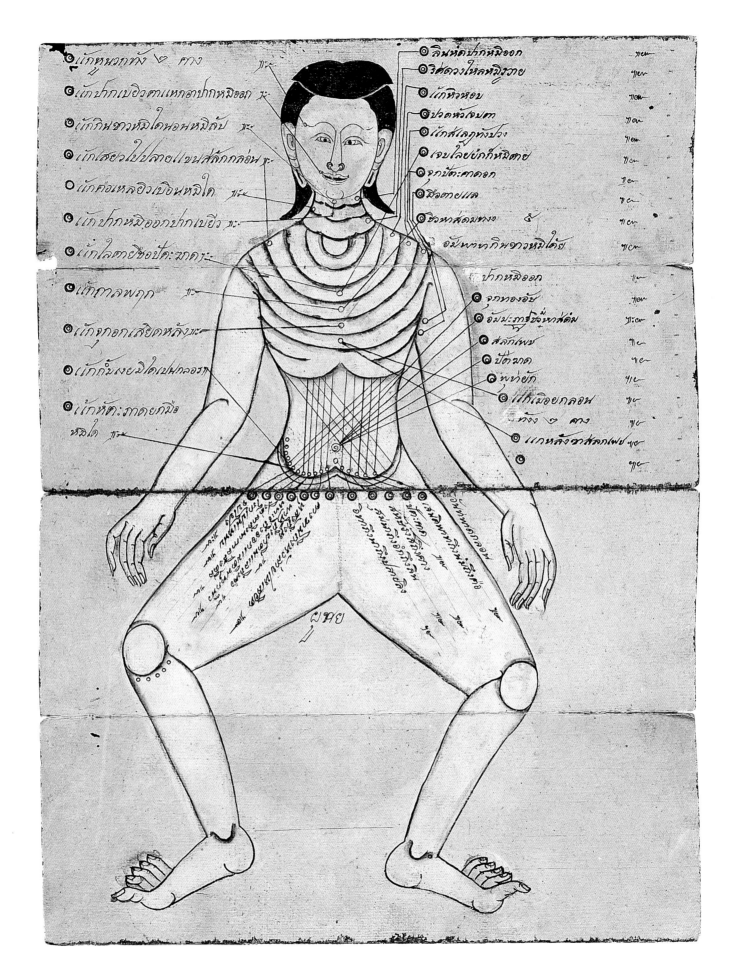

70 The Hermits at Wat Pho, 1838.

Walters Art Gallery, Baltimore w 831, f. 74r.

Folding book manuscript of khoi paper, 39 cm. wide.

In 1838 court artists in Bangkok produced several fine manuscripts depicting hermits performing yogic exercises. The manuscripts marked the casting of 80 large hermit statues at Wat Pho, the royal temple adjacent to the grand palace. They were cast in an alloy of zinc and tin and painted in colours. Although some survive at the temple, many fell into disrepair and were discarded.

   The hermits were part of an ambitious undertaking by King Rama III and his court to make Wat Pho a centre of knowledge of traditional medicine, astrology, religion and literature. Stone inscriptions composed by court poets were set into walls at the temple. In the manuscripts, the inscriptions describing the hermits are written below the illustrations in gold on a red background between fine floral patterned borders. A colophon at the end of this manuscript at the Walters Art Gallery identifies the artists responsible for the paintings in the manuscript as Khun Rochanamat and M'un Chamnan Rochana, the court artists of the 'left' and 'right.' The scribe is also named, Khun Wisut Akso'n, and the year, 1198 in the Chula era, equal to 1838 AD.

The hermit shown here is using a yoga exercise to treat stiffness and muscle fatigue in the legs, according to the text. To the left of the text at right-angles is the name of the author of the verse, Prince Kraisorn Wichit. Although the artist makes no attempt to represent receding space or any background, the skies are rendered in a 'modern' way with delicate colouring that blends into other colours. The wide borders with elegant textile patterns, are like those on the fine dyed cottons produced in India for the Thai market, a frequent feature of fine Thai manuscript illustration in the first half of the nineteenth century.

   A Thai and a Chinese artisan engaged in melting zinc and tin for the statues in a clay tube are also depicted in the manuscript. And a curious final figure shows John the Baptist as one of the hermits, dressed in the garb of the Protestant missionaries in Bangkok in the 1830s.[1] The missionaries had begun translating the bible into Thai at this period, and apparently this resulted in the misconception of John as a hermit wandering in the desert with injured legs.

[1] These figures are reproduced in Griswold 1965, figs. 1, 21. Griswold provides full details of the manuscript and the hermits.

GLOSSARY

ABHIDHAMMA

One of the three main divisions of Buddhist scriptures treating abstract subjects including psychology and philosophy. *See also* CANON.

AYUTTHAYA

The main Thai kingdom, and its capital in central Thailand, from the fourteenth century to 1767 when Burmese armies destroyed it.

BANGKOK

Capital city and dynasty, founded in 1781.

BIRTH TALE

See JATAKA.

BODDHISATTVA

A being who has obtained the supreme understanding of a Buddha but who remains in the world to help others seek enlightenment and release from the trials of life.

BRAHMA

One of the three principal Hindu gods, with four faces. Three are usually shown in Thai art. The inhabitants of the higher heavens are also called brahmas.

BRAHMIN

The highest caste in Indian society. Indian brahmins served at the Thai court as astrologers.

BUDDHA

A being who has achieved supreme understanding of the nature of existence, and passes out of the cycle of rebirths. The passing is called Nirvana, or 'extinction'. There are buddhas of other ages, both past and future. In our age the Buddha was born in India in the sixth century BC and his name was Siddhartha Gautama. The Buddha of the future is called Maitreya. *See also* PHRA SI AN.

CANON, CANONICAL

Sacred writings that form the official scripture of a religion. The Buddhist canon is divided into three sections called Tripitaka, literally the three Baskets.

CHEDI

A monument made in memory of the Buddha, most usually in the shape of a stupa, a tapering structure with a round base and pointed top. The most important ones enshrine a relic of the Buddha.

DEVA (also DEVATA)

Angel or heavenly being represented often with hands together in a respectful gesture. In Thai they are called Thewada, Thep, Theppada, or Theppanom.

ERAWAN

Thai elephant divinity with three or 33 heads, vehicle of the god Indra. From Sanskrit Airavana or Airavata.

GAJASINH

Composite animal combining lion and elephant parts, inhabiting the Himavanta forests.

HIMAVANTA

Magic forests at the base of the cosmic mountain, abode of the *kinnaras*, half-bird, half-humans, *gajasinhas*, and other super-human creatures, and hermits who can reach these lands by practice of meditation. In Thai, Himaphan.

JATAKA

'Birth Tales', accounts of the Buddha's previous lives before his birth as the prince Siddhartha Gautama. There are over 500 birth tales in the official canon, and other non-canonical birth tales. In Thai, *chadok*.

KHMER

Cambodia, Cambodian. Also Kampuchea.

KINNARA

See under Himavanta.

MAHABUDDHAGUNA

Great Qualities of the Buddha. A title frequently given to the excerpts from Abhidhamma scriptures in Thai illustrated manuscripts.

NAGA

A serpent or serpent divinity.

PALI

The language of the Buddhist scriptures, an ancient language of India related to Sanskrit. It originated in the land of the Buddha's birth, Maghada, in the foothills of the Himalayas in Bihar.

PHRA MALAI

A monk who journeyed to heaven and hell, the subject of an influential Buddhist tale translated into Thai from Pali and much illustrated in nineteenth century Thai manuscripts.

PHRA SI AN

Thai name for the messianic Buddha of the future, called Ariya Maitreya in Sanskrit. (*See* BUDDHA)

PHROMMACHAT

Divination or fortune-telling text. (Fram Sanskrit, Pali *brahmajati*.)

RAMAKIAN

Thai literary epic based on the Indian Ramayana. The legend of Rama and his wife Sita, his brother Laksmana, and their conflict with the demon king Ravana of Sri Lanka.

SIAM, SIAMESE

Old name for Thailand, not used officially since the Second World War. Siam is a name used by neighbouring peoples for the Thai, and appears as early as the twelfth century in Cambodian inscriptions.

THONBURI

Capital of Thailand from 1767 to 1781, located across the river from Bangkok. Also spelled Dhonburi.

TRAIPHUM

Literally 'three worlds', the Thai Buddhist treatise on cosmology describing the entire universe, from the lowest hells upwards through the earth to the cosmic mountain and finally a series of 31 heavens.

BIBLIOGRAPHY

Anuman Rajadhon
1969
Thet Maha Chat. Bangkok: Fine Arts Department. (Thai Culture, New Series no. 21)

Bizot, François and Hinuber, O. von
1994
La guirlande de Joyaux. Paris: École Française d'Extrême-Orient.

Blackmore, Thaung
1985
Catalogue of the Burney Parabaiks in the India Office Library London: British Library.

Bowring, Sir John
1857
The Kingdom and People of Siam. 2 vols. London: J. W. Parker. [reprinted 1969]

Bradley, William L.
1981
Siam then. Pasadena: Carey Library.

Brailey, Nigel
1989
Two Views of Siam. Arran: Kiscadale.

Brereton, Bonnie
1993
Some Comments on a northern Phra Malai text dated C.S.878 (AD 1516). *Journal of the Siam Society, 81,1.*

Buddhadasa Bhikkhu
1969
Siamesische Illustrationen der Buddhalehre. Tubingen: Horst Erdmann.

Buddhist Cosmology Thonburi Version = Samut phap Traiphum boran chabap krung thonburi. [In Thai]
1982
Bangkok: Fine Arts Department.

Burgio, Lucia
1999
Pigment Identification Studies *In Situ* of Javanese, Thai, Korean, Chinese and Uighur Manuscripts by Raman Microscopy. *Journal of Raman Spectroscopy,* 30, 181–184.

Caddy, Florence
1889
To Siam and Malaya. London: Hurst and Blackett.

Collins, Steven
1998
Nirvana and other Buddhist felicities. Cambridge: Cambridge University Press.

Collis, Maurice
1965
Siamese White. London: Faber & Faber.

Crawfurd, John
1828
Journal of an Embassy to the Courts of Siam and Cochin China. London: Henry Colburn.

Cruysse, Dirk van der
1991
Louis XIV et le Siam. Paris: Fayard.
1995
L'Abbe de Choisy, androgyne et mandarin. Paris: Fayard.

Duverdier, Gerald
1980
La Transmission de l'imprimerie en Thailande. *Bulletin de l'École Française d'Extrême Orient,* 68, 209–259.

Finlayson, George
1826.
The Mission to Siam and Hue, 1821–1822. London: John Murray.

Flood, Chadin, transl.
1965
The Dynastic Chronicles, Bangkok Era, the Fourth Reign. Tokyo: Centre for East Asian Cultural Studies. 5 vol.

Floris, Peter.
1934
Voyage to the East Indies in the Globe 1611–1615, edited by W. H. Moreland, London:

Gallop, Annabel
1994
The Legacy of the Malay Letter. London: The British Library.

Gallop, Annabel & Arps, Bernard
1991
Golden Letters: writing traditions of Indonesia = Surat emas. London: The British Library.

Ginsburg, Henry D.
1989
Thai Manuscript Painting. London: The British Library.

Gittinger, Mattiebelle
1982
Master Dyers to the World. Washington: The Textile Museum.

Gittinger, Mattiebelle & Lefferts, Leedom
1992
Textiles and the Tai Experience in Southeast Asia. Washington: The Textile Museum.

Griswold, A. B.
1965
The Rishis of Wat Po. In *Felicitation Volumes presented to Prince Dhaninivat,* vol. 2, 319–328. Bangkok: Siam Society.

Guy, John S.
1982
Palm leaf and Paper: illustrated manuscripts of India and Southeast Asia. . Melbourne: National Gallery of Victoria.
1998
Woven Cargoes. London: Thames & Hudson.

Haberland, Dieter
1996
Engelbert Kaempfer 1651–1716, a biography. London: The British Library.

Hall, D. G. E.
1974
Henry Burney, a political biography. London: OUP.

Herbert, Patricia M.
1992
The Life of the Buddha. London: The British Library.

Ibrahim, ibn Muhammad
1972
The Ship of Sulaiman, translated by John O'Kane. London: Kegan Paul.

Kachorn Sukhabanij
1962
Siamese Documents concerning Captain Francis Light, in *Papers on Malay history,* edited by K. G. Tregonning, (Singapore, 1962.)

Low, James
1828
Grammar of the T'hai or Siamese Language.
Calcutta: Baptist Mission Press.

Lyons, Elizabeth
1963
Thai Traditional Painting. Bangkok: Fine Arts
Department. (Thai Culture, New Series
no. 20)
1963
The Tosachat in Thai Painting. Bangkok: Fine
Arts Department. (Thai Culture, New Series
no. 22)

McCarthy, James
1895
Report of a Survey in Siam. London: Privately
printed. [Reprinted c.1985 as: *An
Englishman's Siamese Journals 1890–1893.*
Bangkok: Siam Media International Books.]
1900
Surveying and Exploring in Siam. London:
John Murray.

Matics, Kathleen I.
1979
A History of Wat Phra Chetuphon. Bangkok:
Siam Society.
1992
Introduction to the Thai Mural. Bangkok:
White Lotus.

Mouhot, Henri
1966
Henri Mouhot's Diary, Abridged and edited
by Christopher Pym. Kuala Lumpur: Oxford
University Press.
1992
*Travels in Siam, Cambodia and Laos
1858–1860*, with an introduction by Michael
Smithies. Singapore: Oxford University Press.

Muang Boran
1981–97
Mural Paintings of Thailand, Series. Bangkok:
Muang Boran.

N. Na Paknam
1985
*Khoi Manuscript Painting of the Ayutthaya
Period.* Bangkok: Muang Boran.
1987
*Mural Paintings of the Middle and Late
Ayudhya Periods, Nonthaburi School at Wat
Chompuwek and Wat Prasat.* Bangkok:
Muang Boran.

Ovenden, Richard
1997
John Thomson (1837–1921) Photographer.
Edinburgh: National Library of Scotland.

Pallegoix, Jean-Baptiste
1850
Dictionarium Linguae Thai. Bangkok:
Mission de Siam.
1854
Description du royaume Thai ou Siam. Paris:
Mission de Siam.

Proudfoot, Ian
1992
*Early Malay printed books: a provisional
account of materials published in the
Singapore- Malaysia area up to 1920.* Kuala
Lumpur: University of Malaya.

Ringis, Rita
1990
The Thai Temple and Temple Murals.
Singapore: OUP.

Ruschenberger, W. S. W.
1838
*Narrative of a Voyage round the World
during the years 1835, 36, and 37.* London:
Richard Bentley. 2 vols.

E. H. S. Simmonds
1963
The Thalang Letters, 1775–94: political
aspects and the trade in arms. *Bulletin of the
School of Oriental and African Studies*, v. 26,
596–619.
1965
Francis Light and the ladies of Thalang.
*Journal of the Malaysian Branch of the Royal
Asiatic Society*, v. 39, 213–228.
1965
An 18th century travel document in Thai.
*Felicitation volumes of Southeast-Asian stud-
ies presented to Prince Dhaninivat*, 157–165.
Bangkok: Siam Society.
1987
A Letter in Thai from Thalang in 1777.
*Bulletin of the School of Oriental and African
Studies*, 50, 529–531.

Sternstein, Larry
1985
"Low" Maps of Siam, *Journal of the Siam
Society*, 73, 132–157.
1990
Low's Description of the Siamese Empire in
1824, *Journal of the Siam Society*, 78,1, 8–34.
1990
Siam and Surrounds in 1830, *Journal of the
Siam Society*, 78,2, 90–101.

Terwiel, B J
1983
A History of modern Thailand 1767–1942.
St. Lucia: University of Queensland Press.

1989
Kaempfer and Thai History, *Journal of the
Royal Asiatic Society*, 1989,1.

Thomson, J.
1867
The Antiquities of Cambodia. Edinburgh.
1875
*The Straits of Malacca, Indo-China and
China or Ten Years' Travels, adventures and
residence abroad.* London: Sampson Low.

Wales, H. G. Quaritch
1983
Divination in Thailand. London: Curzon
Press.

Wenk, Klaus
1965
*Thailandische Miniaturmalereien nach einer
handschrift der Indischen Kunstabteilung der
Staatlichen Museen Berlin.* Wiesbaden: Franz
Steiner.
1982
Mural Painting in Thailand. 3 vol. Zurich:
von Oppersdorf.

Wray, Elizabeth
1972
Ten Lives of the Buddha. New York and
Tokyo: Weatherill.

INDEX